NATIONAL FOUNDATION FOR EDUCATIONAL
RESEARCH IN ENGLAND AND WALES
RESEARCH REPORTS. SECOND SERIES, No. 3

TEACHING BEGINNERS TO READ

REPORT No. 1

Reading in Infant Classes

Reading

in

Infant Classes

A Survey of the Teaching Practice and Conditions in
100 Infant Schools and Departments

by

E. J. GOODACRE, B.Sc., Ph.D.

NATIONAL FOUNDATION FOR EDUCATIONAL
RESEARCH IN ENGLAND AND WALES
THE MERE, UPTON PARK, SLOUGH, BUCKS

Published by the National Foundation for Educational Research
in England and Wales

The Mere, Upton Park, Slough, Bucks
and at 79 Wimpole Street, London, W.1

First Published 1967

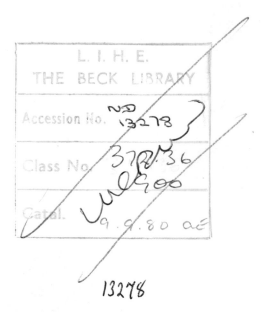

Printed in Great Britain by
KING, THORNE & STACE LTD., SCHOOL ROAD, HOVE, SUSSEX

Preface

THE Infant School or Department is important largely because children spend their first two or three school years there. A growing volume of research evidence suggests that whether or not genuine equality of educational opportunity is open to many children is determined by the nature and quality of their early schooling. There is good reason to believe that the 11+ examination is unfair, not in itself, but because it formalizes a process of selection which may begin at the age of five and which certainly accentuates differences arising outside the school, having little to do with real talent and ability. No doubt the extensive reorganization of education for adolescents will reduce some inequalities and contribute to the development of any reserve of talent there may be. But the heart of the problem of equality of educational opportunity does not lie here.

For reasons which seem to have little to do with an accurate assessment of strictly education issues, contemporary society has focussed its uneasiness on the 11+ examination and undertaken an extensive reorganization of secondary education as the means of reducing inequality of opportunity and developing the nation's reserve of talent. The ongoing research programmes of the N.F.E.R., and child development studies in general, suggest that unless more immediate attention is given to the educational problems of the early years of primary education, much of the effort put into the development of secondary education may be wasted.

Verbal conceptual growth is the basis of intellectual development; and in this, a key part is played by reading, spoken and written communication. It is in the infant school, where for the first time for most children, the professional educator is able to provide what may be lacking at home, that the beginnings of reading are taught. Yet few of those who decry the loss give thought to the educational institution which is concerned with its most critical period of growth.

There are many aspects of the present provision for the education of infants which deserve serious reflection. The schools need new varieties of teaching methods, techniques and apparatus, but the value of these will be minimal unless practical steps are taken based on an understanding of the kind of fundamental factors which determine the child's response to school and limit its progress.

Preface

The attitude of the teacher to lower working class children, the number of terms a child spends in a reception class, the difference in the relation of boys and girls to the women who staff the schools, are some basic factors—an appreciation of factors such as these and an assessment of their influence on pupils' reading progress are essential to the planning for national and local educational improvement.

The present work is the first in a series of publications which will report the N.F.E.R. programme of research undertaken in an attempt to provide some guidance of this kind. As explained in the Introduction, the programme followed directly from the Kent Inquiry, 1954-57; including the initiation of the programme, the planning and supervision of the field work was the responsibility of Dr. J. M. Morris, the Research Officer in charge of the Kent Inquiry. Dr. E. Goodacre acted first as Assistant Research Officer to Dr. J. M. Morris, carrying out a good deal of the detailed observations in selected schools during the period 1959-61, as well as the analysis of the data from the initial survey of 1959 and other essential work. It will be seen, however, that she very considerably developed the original plan and this and subsequent reports owe much to her energy and insight.

The resources available to the N.F.E.R. Reading Research programme since 1954 have been necessarily limited, particularly since the end of the field work when Dr. E. Goodacre was able to give part-time service only; the lack of available resources largely explains the delay in the publication.

The N.F.E.R. is indebted to the London County Council Education Committee for permission to undertake a research programme in the Infant Schools and Departments under their authority; to the very many Education Officers, inspectors, heads and class teachers who not only collaborated in the onerous field work, but who willingly consulted with us at all the stages of planning and conduct of the inquiry reported here; and to Mrs. E. Britton, Miss N. L. Goddard, and Mr. L. H. Quinn for reading and commenting on the manuscript.

W. D. WALL

November, 1966

iv

Contents

of readiness; readiness for what? Teachers' Standards and Expectations: children able to read on entry; reception class teachers' standards; infant school standards. The Use of Standardized Tests: tests used in the infant school; head teachers' reasons for using tests; reception class teachers' comments on the use of tests. Backward Readers: provision for backward readers.

List of Tables

Introduction

DURING the last ten years the National Foundation for Educational Research has conducted and co-operated in several reading inquiries at international, national and local authority level. For instance, the considerable resources provided by the Kent Education Committee permitted research to be undertaken which took the form of extensive inquiries into random and representative samples of primary schools in that county, combined with intensive studies of selected schools and children. The first account of the findings of that research were published in 1959 as *Reading in the Primary School* by Joyce M. Morris. The report endeavoured to answer certain specific questions and to provide a background for future studies.

Previous investigations and the Kent inquiries provided evidence of the close association which exists between high socio-economic status and good reading attainment. Of interest was the report of wide differences in the 'reading readiness' of new entrants, since it demonstrated how unequal is the task of infant teachers working in areas of differing socio-economic status, and the difficulty therefore in reading research of assessing accurately how much progress is due to a school's effective methods or to the contribution made by the home background. It appeared that a logical development of the Kent inquiries would be to institute another reading inquiry, primarily concerned with the teaching of reading of schools situated in areas of different socio-economic status. Also, since the Kent inquiries had been concerned with the reading attainment in the junior department of the primary school, and with the study of the primary and secondary school progress made by good and poor readers, it was desirable that future research should concentrate on the period when the foundation of the skill takes place, the teaching of the subject to children in the infant age range. A project entitled 'Teaching Beginners to Read' was initiated with the co-operation of the London County Council Education Committee in September, 1958.

The broad aims of the project were as follows:

1. To investigate the nature and extent of the task of teaching beginners to read, particularly in disadvantaged areas.

2. To study the reading readiness, attainment and progress of infants in relation to their individual attributes, home circumstances and school conditions.

The inquiry lasted three years (1958-61) and was carried out with the assistance of the Authority's Education Committee and Officers, the Ministry of Education Inspectorate, the Child Development Department (University of London Institute of Education) and psychologists. Altogether 100 infant schools and departments and approximately 5,000 pupils (all born in 1954) took part in the investigation, which was planned in three stages:

Stage 1:   Survey of methods, materials and conditions in
(1958-59)   100 infant schools and departments by means of
             written questionnaires completed by heads and
             reception class teachers.

Stage 2:   A study of particular questions in the schools
(1959-61)   which indicated at the time of the survey their
             willingness to take part in a two-year research
             inquiry.

Stage 3:   Covering the same period, an intensive study of
(1959-61)   central questions in a group of these co-
             operating schools selected to be representative
             of extremes of the socio-economic continuum
             and involving all pupils in the 1954 age-group
             and their teachers, and specifically a group of
             selected good and poor readers.

The findings of the 'Teaching Beginners to Read' project are to be published in several separate but related reports, each dealing with particular aspects of the basic problem. The present publication, the first report of the series, is based on the data which resulted from the first stage of the inquiry (the initial questionnaire), and the 1954 age-group pupils' reading attainment at the end of their infant schooling. It provides a survey of current practice in the infant school. Also, the data has been analysed in relation to the two important factors of school organization and social area in order to discover to what extent these factors affect the general picture described. Finally, the pupils' achievements at the end of their infant course are reported generally and in relation to the two factors.

Concerned as it is with topics examined in detail in *Reading in the Primary School*, the findings pertaining as they do specifically to the infant school, usefully supplement the results reported in that volume. It is hoped, though, that this first London report will be of interest not only to those teachers and educationists who read the first Kent report but also to all concerned with teaching reading from the beginning.

The Design and Conduct of the 1959 Survey

THE survey of teaching practice and conditions was by means of written questionnaires completed by the head and reception class teacher of the schools which agreed to take part in the research when they were contacted as a result of a one-in-six sampling of the Authority's total number of infant schools and departments (607 in all). The sampling procedure produced a group of 181 schools, of which 100 agreed to take part in the first stage of the research. The sampling method and selection of schools are described in detail in the Appendix B, Chapter I (a). The proportion of non-respondents at each stage of the research and the reasons given by respondents not taking part are discussed in the same section of the Appendix.

The original sample of 181 schools was stratified by administrative division and by type of organization with a uniform sampling fraction in order to ensure adequate representation of each type and division. There was no stratification by denomination of school, but the numbers obtained in the original sample were found not to differ significantly from those existing in the total school population. In the Appendix B, Chapter I (b) a comparison is made of the groups of schools which took part in each stage of the research in respect to type of organization, religious denomination, educational division and social area. It was found that the hundred schools completing the initial questionnaires on which this survey is based (100 group of schools), were representative of London primary schools as a whole in respect to type of school organization, and religious denomination. There was no significant difference between the group of schools and the original one-in-six sample in respect to social area, but with respect to educational division there was a significant difference at one per cent between the 181 schools and those completing initial questionnaires. The reasons for two divisions out of the nine being under-represented and one division over-represented are discussed in section I (c) of the Appendix.

In relation to the two variables studied in detail, school type of organization and social area, the survey schools appeared to be representative of London primary schools as a whole.

The survey findings have been reported for the total group of responding schools therefore as being representative of practice and conditions generally to be found amongst urban infant schools. The material has been analysed in relation to two important variables, type of school organization and social background. Pupils' reading attainment (both tested and estimated) in relation to these two variables has been reported in the conclusion of each of the chapters dealing with how practice and conditions differed in respect to the variables studied. Also, whenever it was feasible the survey material was related to the appropriate Kent findings, although it should be stressed that differences between the London and Kent findings may be due to sample differences and differences in the form of the two researches; the London survey was by written questionnaire, whereas the Kent information was based on interview data and observations.

THE VARIABLES STUDIED

Type of school organization

The schools in the research were of two types; infant only (age range five to seven plus years) and junior and infant (age range five to eleven plus years). For the purposes of this report, all schools were recorded as primary schools and their organization recorded as either *infant only* or *junior mixed and infant*.

Social background of the school

This variable was measured by the use of a three division grouping based on the distribution of male occupations within the ward in which the school was situated. The necessary data were obtained from the County Report for this particular Authority which incorporated the 1951 Census figures for social class distributions for individual wards within the Authority. The selection of occupation as the criterion of socio-economic status at that stage of the investigation was based on the idea that in areas of predominantly semi-skilled and unskilled occupations, reading would be a relatively under-valued skill and as a consequence there would be less likelihood of the children from the homes in those areas being easily motivated to learn to read. It was possible to classify the schools on the basis of the criterion into three fairly distinct social areas which may be described summarily as follows:

Social Area 1: a densely residential area, predominantly Lower Working Class.

Social Area 2: also densely residential but mainly Working Class.

2

Social Area 3: less homogeneous than the other two areas, but by comparison, predominantly Middle Class and 'white collar'.

It can be seen from Table I/1 that the largest number of schools was in Social Area 1. This area is the oldest part of the Authority and contains a substantial proportion of the Authority's primary schools, despite the activities of the planners of the school building programme to keep up with the expansion both in geographical and population terms. There was no statistically significant difference in respect to this factor of social background between the original one-in-six sample of primary school and the groups taking part in the research at the various stages. As perhaps might have been expected, there was a higher proportion of junior mixed and infant schools than infant only schools amongst the older, Lower Working Class schools in Social Area 1, but the difference in the proportions was not statistically significant.

TABLE I/1: *Distribution of Schools by Type of Organization and Social Area*

| SOCIAL AREA | ORGANIZATION | | | | TOTAL | |
| | Infant | | J.M. & I. | | | |
	No.	%	No.	%	No.	%
1. Lower Working Class ..	18	47	20	53	38	38
2. Working Class	17	57	13	43	30	30
3. Middle Class..	18	56	14	44	32	32
TOTAL	53	53	47	47	100	100

THE AIMS OF THE SURVEY

It was intended that the information supplied by the teachers in questionnaire form would:

(a) Provide a picture of the current practice of teaching reading in a cross-section of infant schools in a large urban authority.

(b) Supply information regarding the extent to which infant schools of different social background differed in their methods of teaching, i.e. whether schools who vary in the degree to which they are completely responsible for teaching reading, use different methods and techniques, and encounter different types of problems in teaching reading at the early stage.

(*c*)   Obtain information necessary for the selection of the schools for the intensive study.

METHODS OF ASSESSMENT

The questionnaires

There were two types of questionnaire; one was designed for completion by the head teacher, the other by the teacher of the reception class, into which five-year-old children were admitted on enrolment.   Two questionnaires, one of each type, were sent to the 100 co-operating schools.   Among the infant schools were six large schools which admitted the beginners to two reception classes. In the case of these schools, both reception class teachers completed the appropriate questionnaires, but for all purposes of analysis (except that regarding reading readiness characteristics) their answers were combined.

From the co-operating group of schools, 100 Head Teacher Questionnaires were returned completed and 98 Reception Class Teacher Forms.   The two schools not completing Reception Class Questionnaires explained that in one case the head teacher had been unable to persuade the reception class teacher to do so, whilst in the other the head teacher was also acting as the reception class teacher and had chosen to complete only the head teachers' form.

Both forms of the Questionnaires[1] were designed in three parts:

HEAD TEACHER'S QUESTIONNAIRE

Part A: Methods.
Teachers' experience and training.

Part B: Materials, reading schemes, standards, school and class libraries.   Use of tests, head teachers' attitudes to concepts of 'reading readiness' and 'backwardness'.

Part C: Assessment of material and social environment of the school.

[1] The questions in Section A and B, and question (1), Part C, were based on those used in the Kent Interview Questionnaire on Reading, pp. 135-40, *Reading in the Primary School* by J. M. Morris (1959), adapted for use in a written questionnaire.

Part A: Methods, standards, materials, reading schemes.
Part B: Training and experience.
Part C: Assessment of social environment of the school.

In both forms of the questionnaire Part C dealt with the teachers' means of assessing the social background of their pupils, but it was only in the heads' form that information was sought about the material environment of the school. Therefore, in respect to this survey, only question 1 of Part C, Head Teacher's Form, is analysed and presented in this report. Most of the information obtained from the third section of the questionnaires has been used in the second report,[1] 'Teachers and their Pupils' Home Background', which is concerned with teachers' attitudes towards their pupils' home background and the relation of such attitudes and expectations to the level of pupils' attainment.

The data used in the present report is that of the teachers' answers to Part A, B and C (Q.1) of the head's form and Part A and B reception class teacher's form of this initial questionnaire.

Pupils' reading attainment

As has been mentioned, certain findings in relation to the tested and estimated reading attainment of the pupils by the end of their infant course are reported in Chapters VI and VII in relation to the factors of school organization and social area. The reading attainment of the pupils was measured in two ways: (a) on the basis of the teachers' assessments and this measure is referred to as *estimated attainment*, and (b) by the use of a group test of reading attainment and providing a measure of *tested attainment*.

(*a*)   *Estimated Attainment*

This assessment was made on the basis of a 'primer criterion'. This method had been used by J. M. Morris in the Kent investigation and found to be a satisfactory way of assessing levels of reading achievement in functional terms. The teachers were asked to say which book (within the primer scheme being used by the school) each child was able to read at the time the assessment was made. These assessments were made by the teachers of the 1954 age-group children during both the second and third stages of the research (summer term). The findings reported are for the second year of schooling only, when at the end of 1961,

[1] GOODACRE, E. J. (1967). *Teachers and their Pupils' Home Background.* 'Teaching Beginners to Read': Report No. 2. (In the press.) Slough: N.F.E.R.

135 teachers completed assessments in relation to 3,199 pupils. These children were in 63 of the 100 infant departments and schools completing the initial questionnaires providing information on conditions and practice. It will be recalled that whilst 100 schools completed the initial questionnaire, 86 commenced the two-year research programme, and by the end of that period the number of co-operating schools was 65. The representativeness of the groups of schools at any particular stage of the research is discussed in the Appendix B under the heading section I (c).

(b) Tested Attainment

A group test of reading comprehension designed for use in the 1960 National Survey carried out by the National Foundation was given to the London pupils during the summer term of their first and second years' schooling. The National Survey reading test was completed by a sample of 2,733 pupils with a mean chronological age of 7·7 years and a range 7·2—8·2 years. The test was so designed that it could be used with children younger than the first year junior pupils tested in the National Survey. For instance, the test, presented as an eight page booklet containing 30 items of a sentence completion type, only required the children to ring the correct word or words. Early items in the test were printed in large script similar to that used in introductory readers and by teachers on flash cards; the first 22 items were composed of progressively more difficult, alternately phonic and non-phonic items based on a basic vocabulary of words common to three of the most widely used primer schemes. The last eight items were of increasing difficulty in regard to vocabulary and sentence structure. The reliability coefficient on 270 cases was ·956, Kuder-Richardson (Formula 20).

In the London inquiry 3,122 pupils were tested at the end of their infant course in 65 infant schools and departments.

PRESENTATION OF RESULTS

It is on this information that the analysis of the chapters which follow are based. They permit us to develop a broad picture of the problems and successes of teachers and pupils in a variety of areas in London, and to discuss the importance of the two factors—school organization and social background. Finally the implications of these findings are discussed and the direction of future research in the teaching of beginners is suggested.

CHAPTER II

Methods of Teaching Reading

TYPE OF METHOD

THE methods of teaching reading most commonly used to-day are the alphabetic, phonic, whole-word or look-and-say, and sentence methods, so the head teachers were asked to say which of these methods were used in their schools. It can be seen from Table II/1 overleaf that all but four of the survey schools used a combination of at least two of these methods. The exceptions were four schools in which a single method was used, which for all four was that of the sentence method.

Alphabetic method. This method relies largely upon repetition and has been replaced in recent years by methods which emphasize the importance of meaning in the learning processes. In the Kent inquiry, it was found to be in use still; experienced teachers who, having obtained satisfactory results with a previous generation of pupils, continued to use what they considered a valuable method. Similarly, in the London schools some teachers in a small proportion of schools were using this method in conjunction with others.

Phonic method. In its many forms this method gradually supplanted the alphabetic method, and in the Kent inquiry conducted five years earlier than the present survey, it had been found that all the schools in that study made some use of it. Of the London schools, 94 per cent used the phonic method, only six schools relying solely upon the sentence and look-and-say methods, choosing that their pupils should have no phonic instruction during their infant course.

Whole-word or look-and-say method. All the Kent schools had used this method, but amongst the London schools, eleven apparently made no use of this method. It has been held that the whole-word method is particularly suitable for use with the duller section of a class, since concrete words, adaptable to illustration can be used to build up a useful sight vocabulary. Sixteen schools used this method, in conjunction with phonics, so for these pupils presumably the basic sight vocabulary was extended as soon as the phonic instruction provided them with the means to attempt new and unfamiliar words.

TABLE II/1: *Distribution of Reading Methods Used in* 100 *Infant Departments/Schools (Comparison with the Kent Inquiry)*

METHODS	URBAN						URBAN AND RURAL
	Social Area			*Organization*		*Total London*	*Total Kent Expressed as a Percentage*
	1	2	3	Inf.	J.M. & I.		
Sentence only	1	2	1	3	1	4	0
Look-and-say + Sentence	2	0	0	2	0	2	0
Phonic + Sentence	3	2	2	3	4	7	0
Phonic + Look-and-say	5	6	5	10	6	16	15
Phonic + Look-and-say + Sentence	25	17	21	30	33	63	78
Alphabetic + Phonic + Look-and-say + Sentence	2	3	3	5	3	8	7
TOTAL	38	30	32	53	47	100	100

Sentence method. This method uses the sentence as the unit of meaning, stress being laid on the value of contextual clues in the deciphering of unknown words. There were four schools who relied solely upon this method of teaching reading; two schools who used it in conjunction with look-and-say; and seven who combined it with a phonic approach. The group of sixteen schools using the combination of look-and-say and phonics were the only schools to say that they did not use the sentence method generally throughout the infant course.

In short, it seems that the majority of teachers in infant schools use a combination of methods, emphasizing particular ones at different stages of pupils' development. This may be individually assessed or depend upon the teachers' standards set either for groups

8

of readers or for the class as a whole. Because of the popularity of combinations of method rather than any one alone, it appears important not so much to attempt to relate the type of method used to subsequent levels of reading attainment, but rather to distinguish the order in which different methods are introduced to children and to note the stage of pupils' development at which particular methods are most commonly used. The schools can however be divided into those using 'mixed' methods and those, a very small group, using analytic methods. Further, although the majority use 'mixed' methods, even these to some extent can be categorized according to three characteristics: the main method used to introduce reading; and—perhaps the most relevant attribute—the stage in infant schooling at which phonic teaching is introduced and whether or not it is used with all pupils irrespective of individual children's maturation and development.

TYPE OF APPROACH

The heads were asked if the main approach to the teaching of reading in their schools tended to be informal or formal, and to describe their approach as they would if they were explaining it to an interested parent of a pupil.

Educationists believe that it is possible to distinguish two contrasting types of infant school: one which has developed its methods and atmosphere primarily from advances made in the understanding of children's needs and development; and one which is based upon the concept of the teacher as one whose main task is to inculcate certain skills. Distinctions in fact are not so rigid; many teachers recognize the value of a more permissive school atmosphere, and many schools of the second type have adopted features commonly associated with the first type of school. Since the terms 'formal' and 'informal' have been influenced by educational philosophy and discussion, it was considered that the present survey supplied an opportunity to inquire further into what the terms now tend to mean for teachers of modern infant schools.

Of the head teachers asked this question, 73 per cent described their approach as 'informal' whilst 13 per cent said they tended to be 'formal'. The head teachers of fourteen schools preferred not to categorize themselves, stating that they were 'both' or 'mixed'; usually, it seems, because they either started with informal techniques and became more formal in their approach in the higher classes, or because different members of their staffs tended to follow different approaches.

9

In the Kent inquiry, the schools had been grouped as either formal or informal in their approach on the basis of the experience and observation of the investigator, who classified a school as informal in its approach if it tended to recognize the importance of individual differences, encouraged self-discipline, delayed the use of primers until individual children were ready, and encouraged children to learn by the provision of a rich classroom environment. Formal schools were characterized by the use of a primer and systematic instruction from the child's commencement of school, and an authoritarian rather than a democratic atmosphere in the classroom. When the 'mixed' approach schools are omitted 73 per cent of the London schools described themselves as 'informal' whilst 48 Kent schools (80 per cent) were classified as 'informal' on the basis of the investigator's observations. Thus there was no significant difference between the proportions of London schools labelling themselves as informal and the Kent schools so identified. But the picture alters when the London teachers' descriptions of these categories are considered. It was possible to classify these descriptions on the basis of a criterion similar to that used in the Kent inquiry. For the purpose of the London survey the two groupings thus distinguished were defined as:

A *'child centred' definition:* interest being aroused by the teacher using the child's *own* interests, experience, etc.; stress laid on learning through play; the use of analytic methods.

A *'curriculum centred' definition:* child's interest aroused by the teacher, teacher introducing material, likely interests, etc. either through oral or visual approach, i.e. stories, verses, or visual aids; mention of 'directed' play; stress laid on a primer from the beginning; group instruction: synthetic methods.

If the eight schools are omitted who were unable, or chose not to describe their approach, this grouping in comparison with the previous self-labelling type of question produces 38 per cent 'child centred' and 62 per cent 'curriculum centred' schools. If the Kent informal schools are equated to the 'child centred' London schools and the formal with the 'curriculum centred' schools, it would appear that, contrary to the evidence of the self-labelling question significantly more london schools are 'curriculum centred' (0·1 per cent level). This could be interpreted as evidence of a gradual change in educational philosophy and current practice, perhaps a shift in infant teachers' opinions away from a concentration on activity methods towards a restatement of the importance of the basic skills and the value of the controlled and planned classroom environment—a change which is not apparent in the head teachers' usage of the over-worked terms, 'formal' and 'informal', where it is probably the latter term which has become debased by its very popularity. However, as has been stressed in the previous chapter, caution is needed in interpreting the evidence of the two inquiries as, although there is a difference in time between the two studies, they may also involve quite different samples of teachers, since the two educational authorities differ in regard to the socio-economic factor in that whilst London is an urban area, there were both urban and rural schools in the Kent inquiry. Most important of all, the information was obtained in two different ways, questionnaires in London and interviews in Kent.

Table II/2 shows how the head teachers who used the categories—informal, formal or mixed—described their approach in terms of child or curriculum centred characteristics. There are seven uncodable answers, where no characteristics were given and therefore the answer was regarded as unclassifiable, e.g. 'I would not explain my method'. There was one head who omitted the question.

TABLE II/2: *Type of Approach in Terms of 'Child/Curriculum Centred' Characteristics—100 Infant Departments/Schools*

FORMAL/INFORMAL *	CHILD CENTRED	CURRICULUM CENTRED	ANSWER + UNCODABLE	TOTAL LONDON
Formal	0	12	1	13
Mixed	4	9	1	14
Informal	31	36	6	73
TOTAL	35	57	8	100

Significantly more formal methods than informal methods were described as curriculum centred (1 per cent level).

Main considerations dictating the type of teaching employed

The head teachers gave a variety of reasons for their choice of teaching method(s). The mean number of items for the total group of head teachers was 1·4.

11

A third of the head teachers replied that their main consideration was to provide for their pupils' individual needs. This possibly helps to explain the popularity of 'mixed' methods of instruction, rather than the use of a single method which might not prove suitable for all children, even in apparently homogeneous groups. More than a quarter of the heads believed their choice of methods and materials was influenced directly by their pupils' particular social background; either that they were compensating for inadequacies in the home environment, providing the necessary but frequently lacking motivation to learn to read, or that they utilized pupils' home life and social conditions as the basis for further development. Many head teachers demonstrated an awareness of problems (which often they seemed to believe were peculiar to their own school areas), and tried to adapt their methods of teaching to these specific conditions; others, although apparently equally familiar with these external requirements, expressed themselves as much or more concerned with the ability, training and age of their staff, particularly in regard to the effective use of particular methods. A small group (12 per cent) referred to the experience or interest of members of staff in a specific method, but even in this group there was little sign of what one might term the fanatical adherent of any particular method. Sixteen head teachers considered pupils should learn by a method which enabled them to do so for enjoyment and pleasure, and thus gain an appreciation of reading as adventure and a form of communication: an extension of the individual self. Only two heads wanted to cultivate their pupils' taste in reading. Limitations imposed by buildings, size of class, and length of infant schooling were mentioned by fourteen heads, whilst six mentioned that pupils' general level of intelligence was a major consideration.

Remembering that differences may be due to sample differences, significantly fewer London than Kent head teachers mentioned the needs of individual children as a major consideration (0·1 per cent), or the size of classes (0·1 per cent) but more London heads referred to the ability of their teachers (5 per cent) as a consideration affecting choice of method. Table BII/3 in the Appendix shows the distributions of the items described by the different groups of teachers, classified under ten main headings.

Ways in which children's interest in reading was aroused

The head teachers were asked to describe any particular technique or method they had found useful as a means of getting children interested in learning to read. Analysis of their answers showed that the most popular method was that of associating the written symbol with its visual representation—that is, the practice of labelling objects so that children gradually become familiar with the printed word, its distinctive shape and formation, and associate this with its representational meaning. For this purpose pictures, objects and equipment can be labelled, the teacher incidentally or on specific occasions drawing the pupils' attention to their 'names'. The same technique is used in relation to commands and 'action' words at a later stage. A small group of teachers (16 per cent) also used this method in relation to wall stories. These are familiar stories told in illustrated form and placed around the classroom walls. Each picture carries a sentence relevant to the action of the story. The reasoning behind this method is that the children will be attracted by the illustrations and the action will assist them in recognizing and identifying the words underneath each picture. It is, as it were, a permanently open book, and the teacher is not relying solely on the curiosity or interest of the child drawing him to the book corner, but presenting a readily available form of reading matter. This method may be of particular importance in social environments in which books and reading matter are less familiar than the visual communication of television or film. This method usually relies upon the sentence as the meaningful unit, unlike the labelling approach which more nearly resembles the whole or look-and-say method, and it is possible that some teachers consider that the element of sentence approach in the wall story may lead to too much reliance on contextual clues and a subsequent slower development of word recognition.

In social environments where an oral rather than a written tradition is familiar, it may be necessary to arouse interest through the more familiar approach gradually relating the comparatively unknown to the known. There were 19 head teachers who said they told stories, read to their pupils and dramatized material before introducing the written word. Sometimes it is true of this same type of social environment, that in a number of homes there may be inadequate recognition of any value in the acquisition of reading as a skill, and it is therefore of interest that only four head teachers mentioned that one of the ways in which they tried to interest their pupils and encourage them to want to learn to read, was by demonstrating the function of books, presenting them as a source of information and reading as a useful and valuable skill. These teachers were all in charge of schools in the middle class area.

A group of teachers, 26 in number, described how they used their pupils' own interests and activities as a basis for arousing interest, labelling their drawings, paintings and belongings and using such opportunities to draw the children's attention to the relationship between the spoken and written word.   Closely linked to this method is that of the use of news sheets, books or diaries which are kept by the pupils either individually or as a class effort.   Usually after discussing class or individual children's news, the events are illustrated, written about and finally read.   The unit of meaning is invariably the sentence, although it is possible to start with the whole-word approach and lead into the sentence method.   In this context it is again surprising that only six teachers, all from infant schools, referred to the 'home made/child made' book which in many ways seems a natural development from the 'news' effort.   It may be that this is considered to be more important at a later stage rather than in the initial stages of motivation.

There were 16 teachers, mostly from infant only schools, who used projects or centres of interest as a means of gaining the children's interest.   Usually the topic is one familiar to the children, either suggested by the children or by the teacher herself.   Where the teacher is closely acquainted with her pupils' interests, either from personal experience of their social background, close personal relationships, or through the 'news' session, such an approach can undoubtedly help initiate an interest in reading, if the teacher is able to maintain the enthusiasm aroused and successfully relate it to the basic skills.

The analysis of the head teachers' answers suggested that a number of them were describing methods more appropriate to maintaining than arousing interest from the beginning, and in retrospect it must be considered unfortunate that this same question was not also asked of the reception class teachers.

Another aspect worthy of note arising from a study of the head teachers' answers to this question, is the reliance they appeared to place upon the provision of reading material and the implied assumption in their comments that this in itself is sufficient to arouse the interest of the beginner.   The provison of sufficient and suitable material must undoubtedly loom large in a head teacher's responsibilities as an administrator.   But there seemed to be inadequate understanding of the problems of arousing interest in children coming from semi-literate sub-cultures.   Many heads appeared to make the middle class assumption that by supplying the means to acquire a skill, that skill must of necessity seem of value to the child.

Again, the views of the reception class teacher on this subject would have redressed the balance.

Altogether twenty-two different ways of arousing pupils' interest were described. Table BII/4 in the Appendix shows the principal methods named. The mean number of methods suggested by the total group of teachers was 3·0; the range 1-8.

MAIN METHOD USED TO INTRODUCE READING

Although the majority of infant schools appeared to be using 'mixed' methods, there was less agreement regarding the best method for introducing reading. It has been suggested by some experts that it is advisable to delay systematic phonic instruction until the pupils have acquired a good vocabulary and developed a real interest in reading. The suggested order of using methods is

TABLE II/3: *Commencing Method in* 100 *Infant Departments/Schools*

CATEGORY	SOCIAL AREA			ORGANIZATION		TOTAL LONDON
	1 (*N*=38)	*2* (*N*=30)	*3* (*N*=32)	*Inf.* (*N*=53)	*J.M. & I.* (*N*=47)	(*N*=98)
Phonic only	0	0	0	0	0	0
Look-and-say	4	2	7	3	10	13
Sentence	4	4	3	6	5	11
Look-and-say + Sentence	16	9	8	20	13	33
Phonic + Look-and-say	5	2	4	5	6	11
Phonic + Look-and-say + Sentence	9	10	8	16	11	27
Alphabetic + Phonic + Look-and-say + Sentence	0	2	0	1	1	2
TOTALS	38	29	30	51	46	97
No information	0	1	2	2	1	3

usually that of sentence, whole-word and then phonics. The Kent inquiry found that the majority of schools tended to introduce phonics at a later stage, although a small group of schools did start their pupils with phonics. The present survey provided the opportunity to ask the reception class teachers about the procedure they tended to adopt. No school in the London group of schools relied solely upon phonics as an introductory method, although nearly half the reception class teachers made use of phonics in conjunction with other methods, i.e. 'mixed' methods. The remaining teachers preferred to use only the analytic methods following theory by delaying the introduction of phonics until a later stage, or in the case of a few schools, choosing not to use phonics at all throughout the infant course. Table II/3 shows the number of schools using the different methods or combinations of methods.

STAGE AT WHICH PHONICS WERE INTRODUCED

Systematic phonic instruction with five-year-olds

The increasing use of 'mixed' methods, and the possible decline in the use of phonic instruction as a sole introductory method, further emphasizes the importance attached to the question of when exactly in present school practice, pupils are being introduced to phonic teaching and especially whether systematic phonic instruction is used in the reception class. It has long been believed by a substantial number of authorities[1] that a too early introduction to sounds may adversely affect fluency and comprehension at a later stage in the child's development and schooling. In the Kent inquiry this opinion seemed to be held by the majority of teachers and only in six schools (10 per cent) were reception class teachers giving systematic phonic instruction to *all* pupils. In the present survey, the reception class teachers of thirty-seven schools stated that they gave phonic instruction to all pupils.

The teachers were asked to elaborate their answers, and some explained why they did or did not give systematic phonic instruction. Only about a quarter of the teachers gave their reasons, as the majority elaborated their answer with comments either about the type of instruction they gave, or if only some pupils were given instruction, the type of child singled out for instruction by this

---

[1] DOLCH, E. W. (1937). Phonic readiness. *Elementary School Journal*, Vol. XXXVIII, November.

SCHONELL, F. J. (1945). *The Psychology and Teaching of Reading*. Edinburgh: Oliver & Boyd.

TABLE II/4: *Systematic Phonic Instruction at Five Years in* 100 *Infant Departments/Schools*

CATEGORY	SOCIAL AREA			ORGANIZATION		TOTAL
	1	*2*	*3*	*Inf.*	*J.M. & I.*	
All pupils ..	14	11	12	18	19	37
Some pupils ..	9	9	8	10	16	26
No pupils ..	15	9	11	24	11	35
TOTAL ..	38	29	31	52	46	98
No information	0	1	1	1	1	2

particular method. Of the 27 reception class teachers who gave reasons for or against phonic instruction, 18 provided this form of instruction because they believed phonic instruction gave pupils a means of attempting new words, to augment other methods; because the pupils already had acquired a knowledge of the sounds from home; or because phonics could help with spelling at a later stage. The other nine were against the use of phonic instruction with all pupils because, either they believed that this was too difficult for entrants whose first need was practice in the recognition of the shape of words, or they considered that phonic sounding words acted as a limitation to reading for meaning and interest at this initial stage.

Of 26 teachers who gave phonic instruction to some of their pupils, half were instructing only the more able pupils or those who had already acquired a basic sight vocabulary. Eight gave no information as to the type of child who received phonic instruction, whilst the remaining five either instructed only those children already familiar with the sounds from their home experience or those who demonstrated a marked interest in phonic elements.

Of those who gave no phonic instruction to any entrant, there were two who explained that in fact they did give instruction to the occasional child showing an interest in letter sounds, but this rarely occurred. Ten teachers commented that, although they gave no phonic instruction themselves to their pupils, the children would receive systematic phonic instruction at a later stage, usually towards the end of the infant course.

C

The actual form in which this instruction was given varied considerably from teacher to teacher, and only 38 teachers supplied information about this aspect. Of these, six taught the initial sounds first, mainly by medium of word games, such as: 'I spy something beginning with . . . .'; one taught the vowels first; three the sounds and names of the alphabet; five used the words of the introductory book of the reading series; two made use of the lessons on the formation of the letters to introduce the letter sounds; eight said they gave the letter sounds but these teachers gave no details as to order or presentation. It should be noted that of this group of teachers, a third explained that they taught the sounds by means of word building, drill techniques, flash cards and largely used class instruction.

Only 13 of the teachers who gave phonic instruction to some pupils explained the form in which they gave this instruction. Two taught the initial sounds first, six the sounds and names of the letters (in one case during lessons on the formation of letters) and one the vocabulary of the primer. Four teachers said they only taught the sounds incidentally; for instance when they were asked for them in relation to the practice of labelling or writing about the children's own drawings.

Some of the group of teachers who gave no phonic instruction to their pupils made comments to the effect that, although not teaching phonics they took every opportunity (children's paintings, games or news) to introduce sounds informally, or they utilized the lessons on forming letters and pattern work to introduce the sounds as well. Two teachers said they believed children could learn their sounds incidentally as a secondary result of analytic methods.

Change of emphasis in the teaching of reading

The head teachers were asked if a change of emphasis tended to take place at any stage in the teaching of reading in their schools. Three quarters of them agreed that a definite change of emphasis did take place but they differed in their opinions as to the particular stage of the infant course at which it occurred. Some placed the change in the top classes, explaining that it tended to be a replacing of the informal methods of the lower classes with a more formalized approach which they considered was a necessary preparation for the junior school type of work. Others reported the change earlier, describing it as taking place in the middle of the school or half way through the infant course, again mentioning a transfer to more formal methods and emphasis upon the attainment of increased competence in the use of the skill rather than simply its acquisition. A further group said the change of emphasis occurred at different stages for different children, depending on their individual progress and development.

Table BII/5 in the Appendix shows the type of comments made by both those who did or did not believe such an emphasis occurred.

When systematic phonic instruction was introduced

The head teachers' comments regarding the change of emphasis in teaching reading provided additional information regarding the stage in the infant course at which systematic phonic instruction was introduced. By relating their answers to those made by the reception class teachers about systematic phonic instruction and checking this data with the question to the head teachers about reading methods used in the school generally, it was possible to group the schools according to the particular stage in the infant course at which phonics tended to be first introduced.

TABLE II/5: *When Phonic Instruction was Introduced—100 Infant Departments/Schools*

STAGE	SOCIAL AREA			ORGANIZATION		TOTAL
	1	*2*	*3*	*Inf.*	*J.M. & I.*	
In the reception class to all children	14	11	13	18	20	38
In the reception class to some children	8	8	6	7	15	22
At a stage later than the reception class	10	5	7	14	8	22
During the middle of the infant course	1	2	4	6	1	7
Second year of the infant course	2	2	1	3	2	5
Not introduced during infant course	3	2	1	5	1	6
TOTAL	38	30	32	53	47	100

Considering that an authority such as Schonell[1] has expressed the view that in his own experience, 'it is not until about *mental age* 7 (i.e. pupils of 6+ years of above average intelligence) that a child can intelligently make extensive use of the breaking-down-building-up method of tackling new words', it is of some consequence to find that at least some and in a number of cases all the children of the majority of schools in the London inquiry were receiving phonic instruction by the end of the reception class, that is, earlier than the chronological age of six whilst a small minority received no instruction until 7+ years, even if then.

---

[1] SCHONELL, F. J., *op. cit.*

CHAPTER III

Reading Materials and Library Facilities

TODAY there are a number of reading series on the market, and teachers are able to make their choice of basic scheme from a wide range of suitable material. Their choice of scheme is likely to be affected by such considerations as: whether the scheme is based on a particular reading method allowing either a phonic or whole-word approach; it uses a controlled vocabulary; that supplementary books are an integrated part of the scheme; the content interesting to children, and the presentation attractive. The continued use of a scheme in a school seems to be less dependent upon economic considerations than the head's willingness to experiment and desire for a change. Usually the practice seems to be for replaced schemes to continue to be used in schools as supplementary readers affording suitable graded material and providing variety. Recommendations from inspectors and other heads' decisions may have had an influence. It is possible that there are fashions in reading schemes as in so many things.

BASIC READING SCHEME

The Kent inquiry of 1954 showed that the books most frequently used at that time as basic readers in that county's primary schools were those in the 'Happy Venture', 'Janet and John', and 'Beacon' series. The London inquiry made five years later in a different group of urban schools, showed that the 'Janet and John' series reported previously as rapidly achieving popularity, had made even further headway, and amongst these schools was more popular as a primer than the 'Happy Venture' series.

Table III/1 shows the basic reading schemes used in the 100 co-operating schools. It should be noted that four schools did not use a basic reading scheme. Of the remaining schools, 82 per cent used a single scheme and the rest two or more schemes. Table BIII/1 in the Appendix shows the type of schools who were using a single scheme or more, while Table BIII/2 gives the teachers' reasons for their choice of scheme.

21

TABLE III/1: *Basic Reading Schemes Used—100 Infant Departments/ Schools*

BASIC SCHEME	SOCIAL AREA			ORGANIZATION		TOTAL LONDON
	1	*2*	*3*	*Inf.*	*J.M. & I.*	
Janet and John	24	17	21	35	27	62
Happy Way	4	7	4	8	7	15
Beacon	5	5	5	3	12	15
Happy Venture	3	3	2	2	6	8
Gay Way	3	1	0	2	2	4
McKee	3	1	0	1	3	4
John and Mary	1	2	0	2	1	3
Radiant Way	1	0	0	0	1	1
Holloway	1	0	0	0	1	1
Land of Sunshine	0	0	1	1	0	1
Today's Work Play Books ..	0	1	0	0	1	1
Mac and Tosh	1	0	0	0	1	1
TOTAL	46	37	33	54	62	116
Mean Number of Schemes	1.2	1.3	1.1	1.1	1.3	1.2

There was evidence in the later stages of this research that some schools changed their reading schemes during the three years of the inquiry, but these schools were few in number and at the end of the research the picture remained more or less the same, with the 'Janet and John' series in use in the majority of schools. Despite the fact that during this period the 'Beacon' scheme was issued in a revised edition, bringing it closer in line with the format and presentation of the 'Janet and John' series, the latter appeared to be retaining its almost unrivalled popularity with the London teachers.

'*Janet and John*' *Books* (O'Donnell and Munro, 1949)[1]

Head teachers said they had chosen this series mainly because of its colourful illustrations, vocabulary control, and its design which allows for the choice of a phonic or whole-word approach to reading. The schools using this series were asked at a later stage of the research to record which approach they used—the short or long series; thirty-one said they used the short series and nineteen the long, whilst twelve used both series together.

[1] O'DONNELL, M. *and* MUNRO, R. (1949). *Janet and John Books.* London: Nisbet.

The supplementary readers, particularly 'My Little Books', were often mentioned as providing useful supplementary material of particular interest to children.

'The Happy Way to Reading' Series (Hume)[1]

This scheme uses direct methods combined with systematic work in phonics. It has a carefully selected vocabulary and important phrases and words are repeated in different contexts. The teachers who used it were particularly impressed by the subject matter which is based on the interests and activities of young children, and expressed approval of the carefully controlled vocabulary and the useful suggestions for independent and group work. They also mentioned the supplementary readers and apparatus as an additional advantage.

Three of the heads who used this scheme had themselves introduced in into their schools, either having previous experience of it or because it had been recommended by an inspector.

The 'Beacon' Readers (1922, 1938)[2]

During the Kent inquiry in 1954 it had been observed that this series was gradually being replaced as a basic reader by more recent books, but many schools retained copies of the books in the series as they found they made a valuable contribution to any reading scheme as supplementary material. This tended to be the case in the present survey for, although only fifteen schools used the readers as their basic scheme, these readers accounted for approximately a quarter of all the supplementary readers named by the teachers.

Of the 15 schools who named this scheme, eight were using it in conjunction with another. 'Beacon' readers 5 and 6 were found to be particularly useful for the strong appeal of their stories, especially those of a folk nature which were rarely found in any other series. Also the gradual progress of the books in the series, the carefully controlled vocabulary, and the phonic graded material were considered to be excellent reasons for adopting this scheme of readers.

Five schools used the 'Original Approach' (1922) and one used the 'Old Lob Approach' (1938), although this edition would seem to be more suitable for schools with rural settings. Eight schools used the newer editions.

[1] HUME, E. G. (1951). *The Happy Way Transition Reader.* Happy Way to Reading, Transition Series. Glasgow: Blackie.

[2] THE BEACON READERS. (1) *Original Approach* (1922); (2) *Old Lob Approach* (1938). London: Ginn.

Other basic readers

Although the 'Happy Venture'[1] series has a carefully graded vocabulary, teachers had experienced difficulty in bridging the 'gap' between Books I and II, and III and IV, and others thought the introductory books rather difficult in comparison with those in other schemes. Of the teachers who used it, most expressed satisfaction with the scheme, believing it had been proved successful and were pleased particularly because it successfully combined the merits of both the phonic and sentence methods.

The 'Gay Way' (Boyce, 1950-1960)[2] series uses the sentence method and has useful supplementary books to the scheme of planned readers. The 'McKee' series (McKee, Harrison, McCowan, Lehr)[3] on the other hand is based principally on phonic and structural analysis. It had been introduced in schools in order to augment or replace schemes based on the sentence approach. The black and white illustrated 'John and Mary' (Ashley, 1937)[4] readers were used in three schools, either with 'Janet and John' or 'Mac and Tosh' (Ashley, 1941)[5]. The 'Radiant Way' (1933)[6] readers were used in one school in conjunction with the 'Beacon' (Sullivan and Cox) scheme as they had proved popular with the children. The school using the 'Holloway' (Holloway, 1935)[7] readers did so in conjunction with 'Janet and John' and 'Happy Venture'. The only school to use the reader 'The Land of Sunshine' (Pollard, 1931)[8] did so because the reception class teacher had found the simple, gaily coloured pictures useful for the look-and-say approach which she used for teaching reading.

Basic reading scheme in the reception class

As might have been expected the basic reading schemes named by the reception class teachers differed little from those listed by the head teachers. The main value of this question was that it elicited

[1] SCHONELL, F. J. *and* SERJEANT, I. (1939). *The Happy Venture Readers.* Edinburgh: Oliver & Boyd.

[2] BOYCE, E. R. (1950-60). *The Gay Way Series.* London: Macmillan.

[3] McKEE, P., *et al.* (1955). *McKee Readers.* London: Nelson.

[4] ASHLEY, E. (1937). *The John and Mary Readers.* Huddersfield: Schofield & Sims.

[5] ASHLEY, E. (1941). *The Mac and Tosh Readers.* Huddersfield: Schofield & Sims.

[6] THE RADIANT WAY READERS (1933). London: Chambers.

[7] HOLLOWAY, E. S. (1935). *The Holloway Readers.* London: Ginn.

[8] POLLARD, R. (1931). *The Land of Sunshine.* London: Nisbet.

the information that in nine schools a basic reading scheme was not used in the entrants class. Two of these schools were those in which a basic scheme was not in operation at all.

Supplementary readers

Three quarters of the head teachers agreed that they supplemented the basic scheme in use in their school with readers from other series which they named; 13 answered that they used a basic scheme and supplementary readers but did not name the scheme or series. Three head teachers did not answer this question and two of them were those who had previously replied that they used no particular series as a basic scheme. There were seven schools where no readers from other schemes were used to supplement the basic schemes, in most cases because the scheme that had been chosen was one which had its own wide range of supplementary readers.

The majority of teachers used readers from more than one additional scheme to augment their basic scheme. Of those named, the 'Beacon' readers and the 'Happy Venture' series accounted for approximately half the readers used in this way. In some cases, these particular schemes had at one time been in use in the schools as the basic scheme, and when it was changed their readers had been retained for use as supplementary material. Others named were 'Gay Way' (12 per cent of the total group of named readers), 'Janet and John' (11 per cent),' Mac and Tosh' (11 per cent), 'John and Mary' (10 per cent), 'Happy Way' (9 per cent), and 'McKee' (3 per cent).

It was felt by most of the head teachers that supplementary readers were needed to provide opportunities for pupils to practise and consolidate those words already familiar from the main scheme, since they believed that this was the best way to give the children confidence in the use of their skill. The main difficulty was to find readers which were within the scope of the child's reading experience and level of attainment, and yet could provide subject matter of interest. As previously stated, the myths and fables retold in simple language in the later stages of the 'Beacon' readers and the 'Happy Venture' series were believed to fill this role more than adequately. A group of teachers commented on the humorous appeal of the 'Mac and Tosh' series to both teacher and child. Apparently humour is not readily found in most of the series.

Practice of allowing readers to be taken home

The majority of heads allowed pupils to take readers home to practise. Some of these teachers qualified their answers, stating

TABLE III/2: *Teachers Allowing Readers to Be Taken Home—100 Infant Departments/Schools*

PRACTICE	HEAD TEACHERS						CLASS TEACHER					
	Social Area			Organization		Total	Social Area			Organization		Total
	1	2	3	Inf.	J.M. & I.		1	2	3	Inf.	J.M. & I.	
Allow readers to be taken home	22	10	11	17	26	43	8	10	8	9	17	26
Not the usual practice, only on request, when standard reached	7	6	4	9	8	17	13	4	9	13	13	26
Reader not allowed home	9	14	15	26	12	38	14	14	11	27	12	39
No information or no scheme	0	0	2	1	1	2	3	2	4	4	5	9

that this usually only happened when a child had been absent for some time or when a certain minimum standard had been attained. In 38 per cent of schools, the head teachers appeared to discourage the practice. The heads were not asked to explain their attitude, but the reception class teachers were asked to give their reasons. Their replies provide some indication of the attitudes which affect a teacher's decision regarding this practice.

As Table III/2 shows, the reception class teachers did not differ significantly in their answers from the heads as to whether they permitted this practice. Of those who did allow pupils to take home their readers, the majority did so because they considered that this could be a useful incentive, and provide opportunities for further practice of the skill. Some teachers believed it provided parents with knowledge of their children's rate of progress, and that it was particularly useful as a means by which parents could share in the experience and pleasure of their children's gradual mastery of the skill.

The class teachers who did not allow readers to be taken home gave a number of reasons for not adopting the practice. Some considered 'home work' to be unnecessary for their pupils or that they were too young to benefit from practising at home, whilst others expected that parents would buy the reader in the scheme. Some teachers were anxious about the fate of readers if pupils were allowed to borrow school copies, whilst two teachers explained that readers could not be taken home since they were school property. It was the opinion of some teachers that in particular cases, the parents' anxiety could communicate itself to their children and create unnecessary worry over pupils' rate of progress, that in fact some parents would 'push' their children. It was much more desirable for books in the home to be different from those used in the school, thus providing a variety of material on which to practise. Also, it was mentioned that in some cases, there was a danger that pupils who took readers home might be tempted to memorize them rather than practise the skill and learn to read for enjoyment.

READING APPARATUS

A subject which occasioned a great deal of discussion during visits to the Kent schools was the place of apparatus in any reading scheme, particularly material commercially produced. Some of the experienced Kent infant teachers explained that in the past they had often spent long hours in devising apparatus suitable for class instruction and for use with individual children, and therefore were particularly pleased to see schemes on the market which supplied apparatus to be used with the basic primer.

Published or own make

Approximately a quarter of the Kent schools used no published reading apparatus at all. Amongst the London schools, only eight replied that they made no use of this type of material, and two of these schools had stated that they did not use a published reading series as a basic scheme. For the majority of schools, both teacher-made apparatus and that published with a scheme had a place in their reading instruction. Table BIII/3 in the Appendix shows the types of schools making use of the different forms of apparatus.

For individual or class purposes

In twelve schools, apparatus of both types was used for class purposes only. Since two of the schools using only teacher-made apparatus and one of the two schools using only published material, used their apparatus for class purposes only, there were altogether fifteen schools in which reading apparatus was used for class purposes only, and not for work with individual children. In the junior departments in the Kent study, children in 27 schools had very little classroom material and no individual apparatus at all. The larger proportion of junior schools not using individual apparatus reflects the attitude of some junior schools, that the use of apparatus at that stage of the child's schooling is of little use, as the children tend to associate it with their infant classes and hence think of it as 'babyish'. Certainly all the infant teachers in the London inquiry found apparatus essential in their work and all schools reported using this type of material, mostly both published and teacher made, and generally for both individual and class purposes. Table BIII/4 in the Appendix shows the different uses made of apparatus in the different types of schools.

LIBRARY FACILITIES

Schools with organized libraries for infants

It was found that a number of the head teachers of the junior mixed and infant schools had replied that they had an infant school library, when in fact details given in answer to the later sections of this question indicated that they were referring to either the library organized for the whole school, that is juniors and infants combined, or the book corners organized in the separate classrooms. In view of this, only schools where a separate library had been organised in the infant department were recorded as those with organized libraries. Such libraries could be placed in a separate room, a converted space in a corridor, or consist of a portable trolley, but the term 'library' in this context refers to an assortment of library books collected by the staff and children for the use of infant pupils only and placed in a central position in the school. Books suitable for the infant age-range housed in the junior school library, unless made available to the infant classes by means of a trolley for instance, or organized as a separate and distinct part of the junior library, were not considered to constitute an infant library.

TABLE III/3: *Organized Libraries for Infants—100 Infant Departments and Schools*

ORGANIZED LIBRARY FOR INFANTS	SOCIAL AREA			ORGANIZATION		TOTAL
	1	*2*	*3*	*Inf.*	*J.M. & I.*	
Yes	23	23	21	48	19	67
No	15	7	11	5	28	33
TOTAL	38	30	32	53	47	100

As can be seen from Table III/3 two thirds of the survey schools had organized separate informal libraries, but chiefly because this was the practice in the infant only schools. Only five of these schools had not organized a central library but amongst the junior mixed and infant schools, the majority of infant departments did not have the use of a library organized solely for that age-range. Since the infant department in that type of school may comprise several classes or in some cases even a single class, it is not surprising that separate libraries were not organized as frequently as in the larger, single department schools. It should be emphasized that in the junior mixed and infant schools, it is often possible that a well-organized class library or library corner is fulfilling the same function as the central library in the infant school. The lack of organized libraries in the former schools is therefore no indication of the actual standard of the library facilities available in these schools.

Library housed in a separate room

Wherever a school library can be organized as an alternative or supplement to the class libraries, it should ideally be housed in a room kept specifically for this purpose so that children may have the opportunity to browse amongst the books. In Kent only ten per cent of the schools had an extra room which could have been used as a school library, and the head teachers of these schools had preferred to use the additional space for other purposes, such as group work with the backward children. By comparison, the schools in this more recent survey were much better placed with regard to space, almost half those with organized libraries possessing an extra room which was used to house the central library. However, it was the infant only schools which had more space than the junior mixed and infant schools; only six of the latter were able to house their libraries in separate rooms. In most cases the passing of the 'bulge' in infant numbers had left the heads of the infant only schools with more space, and a number of them had used this opportunity to reorganize their libraries in more nearly ideal conditions.

Many of the heads who had no extra room in their school showed undoubted ingenuity in seeking a solution to this problem which was mainly one of space. In two schools the library had been organized in the head's office; in six in some part of the school hall; in six they had used cupboards, folding racks or trolleys which were placed in the less congested parts of the building; in five, a cloakroom, the end of a corridor or an entry vestibule had been converted successfully into well-equipped, relatively spacious libraries.

Availability and type of library material

The head teachers who had organized libraries in their schools were also asked to describe how they did this. The answers were mostly concerned with either the way in which the pupils were allowed to use the library facilities or the grouping and type of material placed in the library.

The usual practice seemed to be that of allocating a set time to each class for their use of the library. In a few schools this 'library period' was taken by the head teacher, who showed the pupils how to find the type of books in which they were interested, and then used the remainder of the lesson to help those children who might need individual or additional teaching. In other schools, the library was available during the daily reading period, or when the children had reached the upper classes they were allowed to use the library unaccompanied during the activity periods. In two schools the children themselves did not actually use the library, since the class teachers preferred to choose suitable books from the library themselves and bring them to the individual classrooms, rather than have the delay caused by taking the children to and from the library.

The library material tended to be of two distinct types, reference or more difficult books which the children would find of assistance when seeking answers to their queries or information about their interests, and a selection of books of varying difficulty dealing with subjects of appeal to children. In some schools both types of material were to be found whilst in others one or other aspect might receive more emphasis. Sometimes the older children were encouraged to take books out, usually for a period of a week.

Home-made books are those made by individual children recording their favourite pastimes and interests, or by groups working on a project, and they are often placed on display in the classroom. In Kent only nine schools did not have a place for the home-made book in the organization of their libraries. In the present survey only one school mentioned this type of material; schools may have used this material more widely than appeared, but it is of interest that such material did not come readily to the teachers' minds.

The organizing motive behind many of these libraries seemed to be to produce in this room an extension of that type of rich classroom environment which makes possible the opportunity for children's abilities to develop freely. The principal function of the library seemed to be to demonstrate that books were exciting and valuable, the means of acquiring desired knowledge, and that this impression could but stimulate the non-reader and tyro alike.

Library books allowed to be taken home

In eleven schools the children were allowed to take their library books home, and in an additional two schools pupils were permitted to take out the cheaper books or those with paper covers. Generally the practice seemed to be for children to learn to use the library and to use the library books as supplementary readers, not as books for reading at home.

Class libraries and library corners

The heads in the Kent inquiry reported that every classroom had its own collection of library books, varying in number and content

31

according to the age and ability of the children, and the amount of space available. In the present survey, ninety-five heads replied that all their teachers had library corners in their classrooms. In three junior mixed and one infant school, only some of the teachers had organized library corners. Three of the schools were housed in particularly old buildings and were overcrowded, so that it was difficult to find the space necessary for a library corner. All three had managed to organize a central infant library, improvising with cupboards, trolleys and part of the school hall. The other school in which only some teachers had provided class libraries also had no central library.

Only one head replied that no teachers in the school had a class library. This also was a school in which the building was out dated and overcrowded with cramped conditions, making space a valuable commodity; but even here an effort had been made to establish a separate infant library in what were very difficult circumstances.

Sources for obtaining library books

The majority of teachers understood this question to refer to their financial sources for obtaining books, although a few interpreted the question as meaning the form of recommendation and cited 'book catalogues', exhibitions, etc. In most schools, the heads used a portion of their yearly 'capitation' allowance for apparatus, stationery and books to purchase suitable material. Approximately half the schools had at some time received a grant from the Authority to set up a library.[1] The general practice seems to have been to use the library grant to establish the departmental or central library, and then to add to it and establish the individual class libraries gradually year by year using a portion of the 'capitation' allowance for this purpose.

The L.C.C. has a well-organized loan service with a variety and range of books suitable for the infant age-group. It was therefore somewhat unexpected to find that only 17 schools availed themselves of it. Whether this is because of insufficient publicity of this amenity by the Authority itself or because of actual difficulties

[1] A five-year capital programme of library development was authorized in 1954. This provided library books, furniture and equipment for schools of all kinds. The initial provision for infant schools was two library books per pupil, but this was later increased to four books per pupil.

involved in the use of the service, is not known. In three schools, the teachers, acting as borrowers, made use of the local borough library as a means of obtaining suitable books.

Only nine schools in the sample had a parent-teacher organization therefore it was not surprising to find that only ten schools mentioned children, their parents or parent-teacher associations as sources of books. In 18 schools, the head and the staff bought and donated books to the library and in 15, the head noted it was their practice to buy library books with any prize money the school received.

CHAPTER IV

The Assessment of Reading Ability

THIS chapter deals with the measurement of the reading ability of infants, a topic which usually gives rise to a certain amount of discussion amongst infant teachers, since the majority usually point out the difficulties involved in testing young children and interpreting their results if standardized group tests are used. The importance of rapport between tester and child is frequently stressed. It is suggested that with infants of this age, group measures may have low reliability and tests of attainment may be affected by such things as the child's emotional development, physical maturation, and the educational philosophy of the school, which may encourage desirable qualities such as friendly co-operation between children and freedom of expression, which can adversely affect the control of test conditions. Those who are critical of the practice of testing young children usually suggest that the assessments of the trained and experienced teacher are a more reliable measure, based as they are on the teacher's knowledge and observation of pupils and their behaviour.

The assessment of reading ability in the infant school tends to be on two levels. Firstly, there are those children who are already able to read and for whom the problem for the teacher becomes increasingly one of the accurate assessment of the level of reading ability and diagnosis of those difficulties which are impeding progress. For the majority of children the initial assessment is that of 'readiness' to learn to read—that is, the degree to which individual children will be likely to profit by systematic reading instruction. Therefore the situation for the teacher is that of reliably assessing the development of those basic contributory skills, such as auditory and visual discrimination, conceptualization, and symbol and meaning co-ordination, which are involved in the total skill of reading. Assessment at that stage is that of testing the level of pre-reading abilities.

In both cases, it remains for the teacher to interpret and act upon the information which such measures provide, and teachers differ both in their desire for such data and their confidence in the reliability of the information. Although the use of standardized tests in

34

schools has increased in the last decade, this report shows that such measures are confined to the assessment of older infants, and that the infant teacher depends largely upon subjective estimates, based on the reliability of her own power of observation, to determine an individual pupil's reading ability throughout their infant schooling.

Teachers' assessments of the pre-reading skills and initial stages of reading ability are discussed first, followed by details as to the use of standardized tests, the establishment of reading standards, and the application of terms such as 'backward' to infant children.

READING READINESS

The concept

During the Kent inquiry, discussions with the school staffs had shown that although the idea of 'reading readiness' was commonly accepted amongst teachers, most experienced considerable difficulty in describing how they assessed it.   None of the schools used 'reading readiness' tests, and teachers tended to believe that its measurement was a matter of instinct.   When pressed to explain this attitude in terms that might be useful to a young teacher from college, most were able to express what they meant more concretely. The most frequently mentioned means of determining when a child was ready to read was the observation of his desire to learn, demonstrated by interest in and selection of a book, coupled with a request for and interest in words.   To these teachers, the assessment of 'reading readiness' was mainly dependent upon the development of their powers of observation, and from experience they had learnt that the possession by pupils of certain abilities and attitudes predisposed them to benefit from reading instruction.

The present survey offered an opportunity to take this question further, and both the heads and those more closely concerned with the problem, the reception class teachers, were asked to explain what they understood by the term and how in fact they recognized readiness to read.   It was hoped that their answers might elicit not only further information about the actual signs of 'readiness' but that this data might be of use in the construction of a battery of Reading Readiness Tests for use in the infant school.

Teachers' use of the term 'reading readiness'

As will be seen from Table IV/1 the teachers attached more importance to attitude and interest in learning to read than to the development of the perceptual abilities as a sign of 'readiness'. If these answers are indicative of practice at this stage, then it is highly likely that this finding has important implications. This will perhaps become clearer if two aspects of the problem are discussed at greater length, e.g. motivation to learn and the development of the perceptual abilities involved in the learning task.

TABLE IV/1: *Characteristics of Development Named by the Head and Class Teachers as Signs of Reading Readiness—100 Infant Departments and Schools*

ESTIMATE OF CHILD'S DEVELOPMENT[1]	% (559 items)
1. *Attitude to Reading Activities* (Interest in all kinds of books: keen to read: interested in printed word generally: interested in pre-reading activities and materials: interested in stories from books).	48.5
2. *Perceptual Abilities* (2nd Stage) (Recognizes classroom words generally: recognizes words out of context: recognizes words from introductory reader: recognizes own name).	13.2
3. *Use of Reading Materials* (Uses reading apparatus correctly: handles books carefully).	8.6
4. *Perceptual Abilities* (1st Stage) (Knows letter sounds: can discriminate shapes generally: recognizes captions to pictures and objects: associates pattern of words with pictures and ideas: is aware of left to right sequence).	7.7
5. *Language Development* (Good or adequate oral vocabulary: fluent, clear speech).	6.3
6. *Adjustment to School Situation* (Emotionally secure and able to concentrate: rich background of experience and information: socially co-operative and adjusted to school routine: physically healthy).	4.8
7. *General Attitude to School Environment* (Makes effort and is eager to learn: interested in class environment and activities).	4.6

continued on next page.

TABLE IV/1—*continued*

ESTIMATE OF CHILD'S DEVELOPMENT[1]	% (559 items)
8. *Intellectual Ability* (Sufficient ability to tackle work confidently: good powers of observation and range of ideas: can think clearly and independently: learns quickly and has good memory: capable of understanding own and others' mistakes).	3.4
9. *Interest in Writing Activities* (Tries and is eager to write).	2.9

[1] In a later stage of the investigation schedules based on these developmental characteristics were designed and used as a means of measuring the reading readiness of the pupils. These assessments by the teachers were completed when pupils were five and six years of age, and it is intended that these estimates will be related to the pupils' scores on an American battery of reading readiness tests taken at five and six. The estimates were completed for pupils in all co-operating schools, whilst the tests were taken only by the pupils in the selected schools.

The relationship of motivation and perceptual development in reading readiness

In the learning of any skill, undoubtedly motivation to do so is important, but desire to master a skill is not enough in itself. For instance, if one takes the analogy of a child wanting to learn to ride a bicycle like an older brother, a desire to accomplish this feat may exist long before the physical maturation necessary to succeed has been attained. In this particular instance, there are several courses of action available for any adult interested in helping the child to further his desire. One can help the child to balance on the seat of the machine and holding him in position, enable him to learn to keep an upright position, to steer the machine and gain some knowledge of road sense (all abilities necessary to the accomplishment of the total skill); or one can buy a smaller model more within his capabilities. In due course a normal-sized machine will probably be required, but the techniques developed and the experience and confidence gained in mastering the elementary skills will be invaluable for the total learning situation. Another alternative is to ban the whole performance, as being too dangerous at that stage, and tell the child to wait until he is older, by which time he will probably either have taken up other pursuits and lost all interest in accomplishing this skill, or have nagged an older brother or another adult into giving him the knowledge or supplying him with the experience and encouragement necessary, according to the strength of the drive to learn. The crucial aspect of all such learning situations is the necessity to maintain the interest to learn, while keeping the learning situation within the capabilities of the learner at that stage. The process needs to be one of constant reappraisal, the teacher providing opportunities for practice so that confidence is gained and the knowledge assimilated, all the while watching for signs of flagging interest or the opportunity to introduce the child to the next task in the sequence. The latter may prove particularly difficult as it necessitates a knowledge by the teacher of the progression and stages of learning involved in the teaching of the skill. Those familiar with teaching machines would recognize this as the knowledge of the necessary units of programming.

Abilities measured in reading readiness tests

The definition of stages and the order in which information and techniques should be taught is in reading particularly difficult since the skill involved is very complex. The detection of readiness to learn is even more difficult and the analysis of the factors involved at this elementary level is still only at a superficial stage, as is evidenced by a study of the changes which have taken place during the last decade in the construction of tests of 'reading readiness'—measures which are comparatively unknown in this country. Originally constructed with items similar to those used in intelligence tests, and in content often highly dependent on the printed word, these tests tended to be primarily measures of general ability, and pupils' scores were affected by the teachers' previous experience and training and the pupils' familiarity with the printed word. Gradually the design of such tests has altered, and the more recent ones are constructed on the hypothesis that there are distinct basic abilities involved in the complex of the skill of reading, and that a minimum level of attainment in these subsidiary skills is essential if effective progress is to be made. There is still considerable disagreement as to the exact nature of these contributory abilities, their degree of inter-relationship and their dependence on physical and mental maturation; but it is generally accepted that such factors as visual and auditory discrimination, the ability to relate meaning and symbols, and skill in concept formation generally, are likely to be involved in the initial stages of learning to read. These are, broadly speaking, the characteristics cited under the heading 'Perceptual

Abilities' (1st stage) in Table IV/1 by the sample teachers. The second stage, 'Perceptual Abilities', represents basically the same contributory skills, but involve a higher degree of competence in their use, since they are being applied in a specific context—in this instance to the elementary stages of actually learning to read. For example, progress has been made from distinguishing between similar shapes, to discriminating between words, which have similar letter patterns. The stage of the development of these 'perceptual abilities' can be assessed along a continuum of successively more difficult attainment within the areas of these specific contributory abilities. This is of course no simple task, as has been shown by the many item types employed in various tests of 'reading readiness'. Theoretically however it should be possible, once reaearch has provided reasonably unanimous agreement on the nature of these abilities.

The desire to learn to read

What is even more difficult is the accurate assessment of the strength of the drive to learn to read. It is usually accepted that motivation to learn to read is closely related to the type of home background, and in section C of the initial questionnaire, teachers were asked for their views about the relationship between home conditions and the level of motivation. Half the teachers believed that a pupil's keenness to acquire this skill was directly related to their home background, and they considered that an important motivating factor was the pleasure and interest which parents themselves seemed to obtain from books and reading.

In the lower working class areas where reading is a less valued skill, pupils may show little desire to learn, and yet they may be sufficiently developed physically and mentally to be in a position to benefit from systematic reading instruction if the teacher can arouse their interest and demonstrate the value of reading. If this can be done and particularly if effective use be made of any signs of a strong oral tradition in the particular community, then a child from a home where reading is little valued, may yet make steady progress within the limitations set by his level of mental ability.

At this elementary stage a teacher's job is not only to recognize interest but to assess the strength of the drive to learn accurately and to channel it into the completion of tasks which are neither too easy nor too hard. The accomplishment of such tasks itself provides a renewal of the drive to learn and the incentive to further progress.

39

Standards of readiness

The replies of the class teachers allowed us to assess their idea of the relative importance of interest and perceptual development to 'readiness'. Table IV/2 shows how the schools tended to fall into fairly distinct groups regarding their definition of 'readiness' and the standard they adopted.

TABLE IV/2: *Reading Readiness Definitions Implying Readiness Standards—100 Infant Departments/Schools*

DEFINITION	SOCIAL AREA			ORGANIZATION		TOTAL
	1	*2*	*3*	*Inf.*	*J.M. & I.*	
Interest only	11	8	8	13	14	27
Full development of perceptual abilities	10	9	4	9	14	23
Interest and perceptual abilities, first stage only ..	8	3	5	9	7	16
Interest and full development of perceptual abilities ..	8	9	14	21	10	31
No information	1	1	1	1	2	3

There were 27 schools in which readiness was described primarily in terms of the pupil's interest and desire to learn; whereas another group of schools, 23 in number, mentioned only the level of development of the perceptual abilities. Since the latter gave as examples, instances in which the perceptual abilities were being applied to the printed word (second stage), it could be argued that in fact, these children were already reading at an elementary level before being considered ready for instruction by their teachers. Apparently these pupils had sufficient background experience, including sensory training, to apply this to the specific situation of interpreting the written symbol, and probably the major problem for their teachers would be the provision of appropriate reading material on which to practise their embryonic skill. The omission of interest is difficult to understand, but this may have been taken for granted. In a written questionnaire it is not possible to verify this. The effort required of the child to learn to recognize and read words and sentences may have been interpreted as interest in itself. During the field work teachers often mentioned to the writer the child who 'tries to read an older child's reader', 'asks what that says', 'asks to be allowed to read to the teacher', or insists 'I know what they say'. These children convince the teacher by their enthusiasm and their efforts; they demand help and instruction from the teacher. These children are then considered ready to read—that is, ready to profit from systematic instruction.

The third group is an interesting one, as although these particular teachers stress the importance of interest, they only mention the development of the perceptual abilities to the level of the first stage. The last group and the largest are those who mentioned both aspects, that is both interest and the full development of the perceptual abilities.

There is very little information available in the answers to this question as to the form of instruction for which the teachers considered their pupils were ready—pre-reading sensory training and experience; formal systematic instruction; phonics; their first primer. It is possible though to make some generalizations about this, if we relate the teachers' answers to their replies regarding the introductory method and systematic phonic instruction in the reception class.

Readiness for what?

There was no significant difference between the schools adopting different standards of readiness and the type of introductory method they used. Whether readiness was recognized in terms of interest only, perceptual abilities only or a combination of the two, similar proportions of children were introduced to reading by either global methods excluding phonic instruction or 'mixed' methods inclusive of phonics.

Similarly, whatever the standard of readiness recognized, approximately the same proportion of schools would within the first year of schooling provide systematic phonic instruction for some or all children.

TEACHERS' STANDARDS AND EXPECTATIONS

From this discussion of the replies to the question on readiness, it can be seen how diverse are standards and opinions as to what constitutes 'readiness'. Similarly, diversity of expectations about pupils may be the explanation of the absence of significant differences between the teachers' estimates of the proportion of children able to read on entering school.

Children able to read on entry

The fact that children came from homes of varying motivation level would have lead one to expect that some schools, particularly those in the less skilled social areas, would have had a higher proportion of pupils unable to read. However the majority of reception class teachers believed that none of their pupils were able to read when they entered school at five, and of those teachers who estimated that some were able to do so, the highest proportion reported in any school was 27 per cent; in a working class area, church school (Table BIV/1 Appendix).

It is probable that different teachers have different ideas of what constitutes 'being able to read' in a five-year-old. Since there were no significant social area differences regarding the proportions of pupils judged by their teachers as able or unable to read at entry, it would seem that the standards applied were more stringent in the more favoured groups. It is manifest too that the majority of reception class teachers consider themselves as in the main responsible for teaching their pupils to read.

Reception class teachers' standards

Since most reception class teachers believed this, it is of interest to know whether they demanded a specific standard of pupils by the end of their period in the reception class. Two-thirds of them were found to set no specific standard; in most cases they believed each child should be allowed to progress at his own rate or that any uniform goal was unattainable since promotion to the next class was dependent upon age rather than ability. In several instances the teacher went up to the next class with her pupils, and consequently felt that in such circumstances standards were not applicable at the end of the reception class period. A few teachers commented that standards were not expected of infants in their first year although specific achievements were required later. Table BIV/2 in the Appendix shows the distribution of teachers in the different types of schools who did or did not set a specific standard for their reception class pupils.

This question was probably more difficult for the teachers in the infant only schools to answer satisfactorily, for these tended to be the larger with more classes, and it was sometimes possible for the children of these schools in certain cases to remain for only a term in the reception class, whereas usually in the junior mixed and infant schools, the reception class teacher had the same class of children for a year, and in three schools, the infant age children were organized in a single class and were with the one teacher for the whole of their infant schooling. The main object of the teachers, who were with their pupils for only a term before they were promoted, was probably to see that their pupils settled down to school routine. They would be satisfied if this occurred and if the children had adjusted sufficiently to make some limited progress.

The reception class teachers, 36 in number, who said they aimed at a specific standard, described it, and their answers are classified in Table BIV/3 in the Appendix. Even when it is remembered that some infant only reception class teachers may have their pupils for as long as two years, the standards described show a lack of uniformity.

Infant school standards

The heads were asked to estimate the progress their pupils would make by the end of their infant course in the graded books of the reading scheme in use in the school. Table IV/3 shows the mean estimated percentage of pupils on each book level, and the final column gives the actual reading standards achieved by the Kent children 1953 at the beginning of their junior school course according to this 'primer criterion'. The estimated book levels by the London teachers were based on the teachers' estimated percentages weighted by roll of infant school or department.

TABLE IV/3: *Mean Predicted Percentage of Pupils on Each Book Level by End of Infant Course—100 Infant Departments/Schools*

STANDARD	URBAN						URBAN & RURAL
	Social Area			Organization		Total London	Total Kent
	1	2	3	Inf.	J.M. & I.		
Book 4 and above	52	53	52	56	50	52	54.4
Books 2—3	38	34	33	34	37	36	26.4
Book 1 and below	10	13	15	10	13	12	19.2

The proportion of children predicted to be on or above book 4 by the end of their infant schooling is similar to that actually achieved by the pupils in the Kent schools. The reading attainment of the Kent school children in the final year of their school course was above the National average in 1954, so it appeared that the London head teachers were setting fairly high standards for their pupils, especially if one considers that they were estimating a smaller proportion of readers at the level of book 1 and below.

THE USE OF STANDARDIZED TESTS

The replies and estimates given above were based on the teachers' own observations and were consequently subjective forms of assessment. Therefore it was decided also to find out the extent to which teachers used more objective measures, such as group or individual tests standardized on general populations of children. The head teachers were asked if they used any tests in their school or department and if so why they used them, and the reception class teachers were asked if they used tests and to name them if they did so.

Tests used in the infant school

It is held by many that tests of attainment are out of place in an infant school and no test of reading attainment is usually given until at least the end of the first year in the junior school. The use of standardized tests has however grown generally in popularity during the last few years, and it is not surprising to find that 43 per cent of the schools in the present survey used such tests.

TABLE IV/4: *Heads using Tests in the Infant School—100 Infant Departments/Schools*

USE OF TESTS	SOCIAL AREA			ORGANIZATION		TOTAL
	1	2	3	Inf.	J.M. & I.	
Using tests	17	16	10	20	23	43
Not using tests	21	14	22	33	24	57

Five head teachers noted that they used the test they mentioned only occasionally. Of those using tests, 40 per cent did so only in the last term before promoting pupils to the junior school. Six heads, although stating that they did not use tests, made a point of mentioning that they recorded the pupils' progress by testing them for their knowledge of letter sounds or recognition of the words of the basic vocabulary of the primer. That testing was still not completely accepted by all head teachers as time well spent, was evidenced by the attitude of the respondent who stated that she thought 'it was better to help the children learn to read than spend time testing'. As can be seen from Table BIV/4 in the Appendix, Schonell's tests were the most often mentioned; more than half of the schools using standardized tests used this particular one. Eleven schools employed Burt's Graded Word Reading Test[1] and six the Holborn Reading Scale (Watts).[2] The Analysis of Reading Ability by M. D. Neale[3] although only published in 1958 was already being tried by one school where the headmaster was particularly interested in measures of reading attainment. Only three schools were using two different types of reading attainment test although in recent years this practice has been suggested as advisable. Tests such as those of Schonell and Burt are measures of word recognition, and in order to gain a reliable assessment of a pupil's reading ability, it is usually considered that the scores of these tests should be compared with those of a test which emphasizes reading for meaning, such as the Holborn Scale, in order that a more rounded picture of the pupil's reading attainment may result.

Head teachers' reasons for using tests

The majority of heads used reading tests to gain an objective measure of an individual pupil's reading abilities, either so that they could place each child with some accuracy in a reading group appropriate to his level of attainment, or in order to assess a child unfamiliar to them, such as one transferred from another school. In four schools, the results were not used by the head teachers themselves but were forwarded to the heads of the junior schools at the time of transfer to assist the latter in organizing their first year classes. The heads of eight schools used the information as a guide to selecting children in need of special help and attention in their last year in the infant school, either by reason of their above average abilities, or their backwardness. In three schools the head teacher

---

[1] BURT, *Sir* CYRIL. The Burt (Re-arranged) Word Reading Test. London: University of London Press.

[2] WATTS, A. F. The Holborn Reading Scale. London: Harrap.

[3] NEALE, M. D. (1958). *Analysis of Reading Ability*. London: Macmillan.

had introduced tests so as to ascertain the progress being made by the children in each class, and then give assistance to the teachers who had children in need of special attention.

Reception class teachers' comments on the use of tests

No reception class teacher used a standardized reading test, but fourteen teachers explained how they tested pupils at this age. Twelve tested word recognition by asking the children to name the words provided in the vocabulary lists in the back of the primer, or on flash cards, wall charts, or other reading apparatus. Only one teacher tested for the knowledge of the letter sounds, and one teacher used the Beacon Book 1 and 2, 'Getting Ready for Reading' which includes pre-reading sense training exercises. Seven of the reception class teachers commented that they considered testing was of no value at this age.

BACKWARD READERS

These London heads were asked whether they considered the term 'backward' could be applied to infant children. There was no significant difference between the answers of those who used standardized tests and those who did not, 55 per cent of all heads thought the term could be applied to children under the age of seven. This is in contrast to the opinions of the Kent teachers[1] who considered the poor or non-reader a problem at any age, but were rather cautious about using the term 'backward' in relation to children under seven. Cases were quoted of children who appeared to be making little or no progress with reading during the first part of the infant course who began to develop rapidly towards the end of it. The Kent teachers were generally of the opinion that seven plus, which tends to mark the beginning of more formal work for most children, was the earliest appropriate age for diagnosing and treating backwardness in reading.

At least half of the London teachers who considered the term could be applied to infants gave their reasons for their opinion. Five used the term because they felt that any child who could not keep up with the work of a class of his own age was, in comparison with his peers, unable to progress and therefore backward. Ten expressed views similar to those of the Kent teachers, saying a child

---

[1] It will be recalled that the Kent teachers gave their opinions orally to the research worker, whereas in the present survey the teachers answered a written questionnaire.

TABLE IV/5: *Heads who Believed Term 'Backward' Applicable to Infants*—100 *Infant Departments/Schools*

CATEGORY	SOCIAL AREA			ORGANIZATION		TOTAL
	1	*2*	*3*	*Inf.*	*J.M. & I.*	
Term applicable	22	16	17	32	23	55
Term not applicable ..	16	14	15	21	24	45

was correctly termed backward if no attempt had been made to learn to read by the age of 7 or 7+ years, since it was considered normal for the majority of children to have started by that age. If a child had been a poor attender at school or entered late he would be 'backward' in the opinion of four teachers, whilst deficient mental ability was thought to result in 'backwardness' in the view of four others. Eight teachers considered the term could be applied to children with special difficulties or those described as 'having got off to a slow start'. Three head teachers of lower working class schools expressed the belief that children who came from homes with few books or where one of several factors could affect the rate of progress long before the children came to school, could be described as 'backward'.

Some of the heads who were of the opinion that the term was not applicable to infant school children, continued to explain that they preferred to use the 'less hopeless' term of 'slow or late developer'. Two teachers considered the term unsuitable since it could not fairly be applied to children coming from a diversity of home background, in which physical, social and emotional factors could vary considerably in their effects.

One head thought the term should not be used whilst there were staffing difficulties and the existence of large classes, whilst another believed it was not applicable to children at this stage of development.

Provision for backward readers

Although there was lack of agreement amongst the heads as to whether the term was really applicable to infants, it was of interest to know whether they made any special provision for backward readers irrespective of their opinion. The head teachers were asked for this information, and where they replied that the class teacher relied on the effectiveness of using individual teaching and gave help to the slower children only within the period of instruction allocated for reading, this was not recorded as constituting special provision for these children. Table IV/6 shows that more than half the schools did in fact make special provision for these children: either in the form of the head teachers themselves taking groups of individual children in need of extra help for specific periods daily, or when they had the opportunity to do so; or in those schools which had the help of a part time teacher, small groups of pupils were organized and taken by this teacher for set periods each day, or for part of a day once a week. Four heads chose to take the major part of the class themselves, the good and average readers, for some of the reading periods during the week, thus enabling the class teacher to concentrate on those pupils in need of special attention. In only two schools, situated in working and middle class areas respectively, did the head teachers mention seeking the help of the parents of the children considered to be 'backward' in reading.

TABLE IV/6: *Special Provision for 'Backward' Readers—100 Infant Departments/Schools*

PROVISION	SOCIAL AREA			ORGANIZATION		TOTAL
	1	*2*	*3*	*Inf.*	*J.M. & I.*	
Yes	18	16	18	37	15	52
No	20	14	14	16	32	48

Seventeen schools were fortunate enough to have the services of an additional member of staff, and this enabled them to organize special lessons for their 'backward' readers. This was in complete contrast to the Kent inquiry in which the head teacher of only one school, the biggest in that sample, had the services of a teacher who was able to remain unattached to a particular class, giving individual attention to the more seriously retarded children, in that particular case, aged seven to eleven. In the different social areas of London, eight schools in the lower working class areas (24 per cent of those schools), five in the working class areas (17 per cent), and four in the middle class areas (13 per cent) used the services of an additional teacher in this manner.[1]

There was no significant difference between teachers who thought that the term 'backward' was applicable to infants and those who thought the term was not applicable, with respect to whether or not provision was made.

[1] No detailed study of the help given by these additional teachers was made; neither were their qualifications investigated.

CHAPTER V

School Conditions

IN the Kent study the school and its neighbourhood were selected for special attention, and the only individual variables considered were the age, sex and non-verbal ability of the children. The sampling design of that inquiry took into account two of the environmental variables studied, the factors of urban-rural locality and type of school organization; and the other environmental characteristics studied were the socio-economic status of the school catchment area, size of school, type of buildings, size of classes and methods of teaching reading to infants. So far in the present report we have been concerned with reporting the methods and practices being used to teach beginners to read, but before examining methods and pupils' attainment in relation to the two important environmental variables of school social area and type of organization, it is desirable to look at the subject of conditions of teaching reading, and under this heading, three of the Kent environmental characteristics are examined. These are school buildings or the material environment of the pupils, the size of the school, and the teacher-pupil ratio. In the present inquiry, it was possible also to obtain information about the training and experience of the staff.

The Kent inquiry found that large schools tended to have superior buildings and unfavourable teacher-ratio. These findings confirmed the association previously reported by Kemp[1] between large enrolment and attainment, but conflicted with his conclusion that good buildings bore little relation to the level of school attainment. In both studies relatively large classes seemed to have no deleterious effect on reading attainment.

MATERIAL ENVIRONMENT

In section C of the initial questionnaire sent to the head teachers, questions were asked about the material environment of their schools. Information was sought on such things as the age of the building, whether alterations had been made, the type of location,

---

[1] KEMP, L. C. D. (1955). 'Environmental and other characteristics determining attainment in primary schools'. *Brit. J. Educ. Psychol.*, XXV, 67-77.

E

and amenities such as hot water and cloakroom facilities. These questions were based on a schedule used in the Kent research. From these data it was possible to provide a total score for each school. The method of calculating these scores is shown in the Appendix.

Age of the building

Table V/1 shows the mean age in years of school buildings for the total group of infant schools and departments, and for the different groups of schools. The average school building was over half a century old. Although buildings were old, often alterations had been carried out which brought the interior if not the exterior of the building up to date, and made for more pleasant working conditions both for teachers and pupils. However, the design of old buildings, particularly those erected towards the end of the last century, often made improvements in sanitary conditions difficult to carry out, whilst high pitched roofs and badly sited windows of poor design rendered conservation of heat in the classrooms particularly difficult. Buildings erected for schools when conditions of teaching were very different from those considered desirable to-day, may be a very real liability and act as a limitation upon the use of teaching methods and experimental techniques.

TABLE V/1: *Mean Age in Years of School Buildings*—100 *Infant Departments/Schools*

	SOCIAL AREA			ORGANIZATION		TOTAL
	1	*2*	*3*	*Inf.*	*J.M. & I.*	
Mean	62·65	63·07	52·91	54·90	64·72	59·56
Standard Error ..	4·76	6·08	6·26	4·08	5·12	3·26

Appearance and location of school

It is almost certainly the intractability of the buildings built for the needs of a different school population which caused two out of three heads to describe their schools as unattractive. Some of these teachers did explain that, although generally the total impression was one of unattractiveness and drabness, the exterior of a school was not necessarily indicative of the interior, and classrooms with cheerful and bright surroundings could be found in the most unprepossessing of buildings.

The same proportion of heads considered their schools were not well located so far as the openness and suitability of the site were concerned.

Facilities

Almost every school had a staffroom (94 per cent) but only 43 per cent of schools had a hall that was used only for assemblies and not as a classroom or canteen. In regard to classrooms 59 per cent of heads considered their rooms were adequate regarding size, with good windows and lighting, and 85 per cent had modern chairs and tables suitable for infant use. Most teachers considered more rooms could have sinks, an amenity which has become more desirable as infant practice has changed; but again the design of school buildings and plumbing conditions are considerations related to the feasibility of installing such desirable but not essential facilities. The majority of teachers reported that they were satisfied with storage facilities and had sufficient stock rooms and cupboards.

Amenities

Both satisfactory sanitation and hot water were reported in 66 per cent of schools, and where sanitation was still considered bad, improvements had been made by the installation of hot water at least. Only in 5 per cent of schools were both bad sanitation and no hot water reported. Schools were not so well equipped in regard to cloakrooms: forty-one per cent reported that they had a separate room with pegs, and a further 22 per cent had pegs and also lockers for the pupils' belongings, but in 37 per cent of schools, the children's outdoor clothing was kept either in corridors or in the classrooms. This is another example of the raising of school standards in relation to material requirements. Improved health standards stress the importance of the provision of hot water for washing. Poor sanitation consists more often than not of badly sited toilets, particularly out of doors, away from washing facilities. Again such conditions may be related to the original design and layout of the school building, and improvements would involve major structural alterations.

In 54 per cent of schools, the infants had a separate playground for their sole use. In 46 per cent, mostly the junior mixed and infant schools, the infants played in an area with the bigger children, and in certain cases this was in very cramped conditions.

Table BV/1 in the Appendix shows the distributions of school facilities and amenities amongst the different groups of schools.

Material environment scores

Table V/2 shows the mean scores of the different groups of schools. A maximum total of 29 could be scored for the existence of desirable characteristics.

TABLE V/2: *School Material Environment Scores—100 Infant Departments/Schools*

	SOCIAL AREA			ORGANIZATION		TOTAL
	1	*2*	*3*	*Inf.*	*J.M. & I.*	
Mean	17·03	17·47	18·66	18·36	16·91	17·68
Standard Error ..	0·51	0·84	1·00	0·61	0·66	0·45
Standard Deviation	3·11	4·58	5·67	4·42	4·53	4·51

It is interesting to note that there were no significant differences between the means of the different groups, but there was a significant difference in the variances between social areas.

SIZE OF SCHOOL AND TEACHER RATIO

The distribution of the different sizes of school in the study are shown in Table BV/2 in the Appendix, and the mean number of pupils per teacher in the different types of schools in Table BV/3 in the same section. The mean size of school for the total group of schools was 118 pupils, whilst the mean number of pupils per teacher was 34·10. There were significant differences between the infant only and junior mixed and infant schools in relation to size, and between the schools of different social area in respect to the factor of teacher ratio.

Age and maritial status distributions

Information was obtained not only about the size of the school and the number of teachers, but also details as to the sex, age, marital status, training and experience of the members of staff.

There was a total of 416 teachers employed in the hundred co-operating schools, of which approximately two-thirds were teaching in the infant only type schools. Of the one hundred heads, 21 were men and 79 women; all class teachers were women teachers.

It was considered of interest to discover whether the staff of the different types of schools differed greatly in respect to the two factors of age and marital status, since during visits and discussion with the teachers during the field work, the impression had been gained that schools in the different social areas experienced particular problems by reason of differences that existed in the age and marital status of the staff they recruited. For instance married teachers are said to be increasingly returning to the teaching profession after marriage, but because of the demands made by their responsibilities, it is probably necessary for them to seek employment near to their homes, and it is more than likely that since they are probably living in the better class residential areas, they will not be interested in the posts advertised in lower working class areas. Also, since infant teaching demands an understanding of the needs of young children, it is often suggested that this type of teaching will be of particular appeal to the married teacher who can draw upon her personal experience of bringing up a family. It was hoped that the data supplied by the head teachers would provide some indication of the extent to which infant schools today do tend to be staffed by married women teachers. The competition for posts within the different social areas must to some extent be affected by the supply of married women teachers, and it is possible that the young teacher straight from training college will experience less competition if seeking a post in the lower working class areas. In some cases, young teachers may even be actively encouraged by the educational divisions and training colleges to apply for posts in those areas where it is known that teachers are in great demand. A staff consisting largely of very young teachers can create specific problems in itself, not only because they are less experienced but because, since the age of marriage is gradually falling, staffing may become unstable simply because young women leave to get married and start their own families. Older teachers on a staff, not only tend to be more experienced, even if sometimes set in their ways, but their very presence over a period of time ensures stability for the school.

Table BV/4 in the Appendix shows the distribution of staff by age and marital status. Almost half the teachers serving in these infant schools or departments were married, and a high proportion were in the years when they were likely to have young families. There are differences between the schools in the three social areas and between the two types of organization. These will be more fully discussed in the next two chapters.

TEACHERS' TRAINING AND EXPERIENCE

The heads were asked about the training and experience of their staff, and the reception class teachers for details of their own training and experience.

Table V/3 shows that the majority of teachers in these infant schools had been trained to teach this particular age of children, and the number of teachers who had more than a year's experience of teaching infants.[1]

TABLE V/3: *Training and Experience of Infant Staff—100 Infant Departments/Schools*

NUMBER OF TEACHERS TRAINED TO TEACH INFANTS

	Social Area			Organization		Total
	1	2	3	Inf.	J.M. & I.	
Trained	132	119	110	245	116	361
Not trained	25	16	4	36	19	55

NUMBER OF TEACHERS WITH MORE THAN ONE YEAR'S EXPERIENCE OF INFANT WORK

More than one year ..	134	120	114	248	120	368
Less than one year	23	15	10	33	15	48

The differences between the groups of schools in respect to staff training and experience were not statistically significant but there are several points about teachers' training and experience which are discussed in the two chapters dealing with the relationship of school organization and area.

[1] It is of interest in this context to report some of the findings of the second report which deals with teachers' attitudes and which includes the analysis of teachers' answers to a personal questionnaire. The teachers were heads and class teachers and they were asked about their training experience and teaching service. It was found that significantly more class than head teachers had been trained for infant work and had more than one year's experience of teaching infants. It was also found that more class teachers in infant only schools had less than one year's experience, fewer of these teachers had one to six years' experience, but also more infant only teachers had more than 20 years' experience; that is, the infant only schools tended to have more young teachers straight from college or only recently trained and more teachers with a long experience of infant work.

Importance attached to the reception class

One of the findings of the Kent inquiry was that although pupils' standards of achievement at seven years of age varied from school to school and area to area, about 45 per cent of the children still needed the kind of teaching associated with the infant school at the time of their transfer to the junior school. Investigation revealed however, that approximately 75 per cent of the first year junior teachers had no training in infant methods, 51 per cent had no experience in an infant school and about 18 per cent of them were neither familiar with infant methods nor had any knowledge of teaching reading from the beginning. Since in the junior school, the staffing of the transition class presented such difficulties, it was decided to inquire in the present survey whether the reception class, the first year of the infant school, was similarly affected with regard to staffing difficulties. As the transition class in the junior school is the link between the infant and junior schools with their different approaches, techniques and standards, so the reception class is the bridge between home or nursery school or class, and the aims and objects of the infant school proper.

It has sometimes been suggested that heads differ in the importance they attach to the work of the reception class and in their concept of its function in the hierarchy of the infant school classes. To some extent the staffing of this class can provide an indication of the head's attitude with regard to this matter. Where the reception class is seen merely as an extension of the undirected play activities of the home and a temporary 'settling in' period in the infant school life of the pupil, the experienced and trained teachers may be given the classes of older children and the reception class placed in the hands of a young teacher. Her duties will be predominantly 'child minding' ones such as teaching the children to dress themselves and develop a degree of physical and emotional independence before being promoted to the higher classes where training and formal learning commence. In comparison with this view, is that of those heads who prefer to place their experienced teacher in charge of this class, because the reception class should provide a rich environment in which pupils can freely develop under the observation of a trained teacher able to detect and direct to some extent the initial efforts made by pupils towards learning the basic skills.

Training and experience of the reception class teacher

Only a small proportion of the teachers employed in the survey schools were untrained, and in only eight schools had the reception class been given to one of these teachers.

Most heads seemed to agree upon the necessity for the reception class teacher to be trained in infant method, but some educationists would agree that teaching experience is equally important. The next step in the analysis was, therefore, to find out in which schools the reception class children were being taught by comparatively inexperienced teachers.

In nine per cent of the survey schools the reception class teacher, although trained to teach infants, was in her first year out of training college, and both teacher and pupil in these circumstances were unfamiliar with school regime (Table V/4). Somewhat surprising is the proportion of teachers with more than twenty years service in infant schools who were in charge of reception classes. Certainly these teachers must be able to bring to the situation invaluable experience, but one wonders in how many cases the boisterous energy of such very young children taxes the patience and reserves of physical energy of these somewhat older teachers.

TABLE V/4: *Training and Length of Service of Reception Class Teachers*—100 *Infant Departments/Schools*

TRAINING	SOCIAL AREA			ORGANIZATION		TOTAL
	1	*2*	*3*	*Inf.*	*J.M. & I.*	
Trained	36	26	28	49	41	90
Not trained	2	3	3	3	5	8

LENGTH OF SERVICE	SOCIAL AREA			ORGANIZATION		TOTAL
	1	*2*	*3*	*Inf.*	*J.M. & I.*	
First year of teaching ..	5	3	1	4	5	9
1—5 years	11	8	10	16	13	29
6—20 years	16	13	13	19	23	42
More than 20 years ..	6	5	7	13	5	18
No questionnaire	0	1	1	1	1	2

As infant school experience or training is needed by the teacher of the transition class in the nursery school, so nursery experience can be useful to the reception class teacher, enabling her to draw upon this knowledge when teaching five-year-olds of different rates of development. In the present survey it was found that only one in four of the reception class teachers did in fact have this type of experience. Table BV/5 in the Appendix shows the number of teachers with such experience, whilst BV/6 analyses the teachers' opinions regarding the effects and observed differences of children having attended a nursery school or class. Of those teachers who had nursery pupils in their class, three quarters believed there were noticeable differences between children who had or had not attended a nursery. Only one in four of these teachers thought the differences were unfavourable, stating that such children tended to be excitable or boisterous, taking longer to settle into the class routine. Most of the teachers considered that nursery experience made pupils more independent and confident, more sociable and responsible and that in their opinion such children tended to settle down more easily on beginning school. Generally infant teachers seemed to be favourably disposed towards pupils having nursery experience, but there was a small group of teachers who were not so sure that the experience was beneficial.

CHAPTER VI

School Organization

THE children in the London inquiry were attending schools of two different types of organization; either a separate infant only school age range five to seven years or the department of a junior mixed and infant school taking children from seven to eleven years. In the latter type of school both the infant and junior departments are supervised by the same head teacher.

The trend since the war has been to provide primary education in separate infant and junior schools. One might at first suppose density of population is the sole determining factor for preferring one type of school to the other, but since the tendency for more children to be educated in separate schools is almost as marked in rural as in urban areas,[1] there are probably other less obvious reasons. However, whatever these reasons are, it is certainly true that an increasing number of five to seven-years-old today receive their schooling in separate infant schools, although it has long been argued that the junior mixed and infant type of organization offers the great psychological and educational advantages of continuity eliminating as it does a break at seven. The infant and junior schools facilitate continuity of methods, liaison between the top infant and first teachers if actually within the same building, and make teaching apparatus associated with the infant level available for use with that small proportion of junior children who may still need it. The retention of emotionally immature pupils who would benefit from a further term or even a year in the infant department, is also administratively easier.

Such evidence as we have of differences in levels of attainment of children in the two types of organization tends to contradict this view at first sight. The attainment of children who have passed into separate junior schools is superior to those of their fellows in junior with infant. However, the Kent inquiries which provide this evidence also showed that the separate junior schools were generally larger, had superior buildings, and were situated in neighbourhoods of high socio-economic status. Hence the apparent

---

[1] PIDGEON, D. A. (1959). 'School type differences in ability and attainment'. *Educational Research*, Vol. 1, No. 3, pp. 62-71.

superiority in performance of pupils attending separate junior schools may not be related entirely to the type of school organization, but rather to the fact that the separate type of school for infants or juniors has been built mainly within the last decade, in the newer housing estates and better social areas, and are thus likely to have a higher proportion of more able children.

It was desirable in the light of this to discover whether these same trends were to be found in the present inquiry. From the present data the fact emerges that in the London area at any rate, this association does not hold completely. There is no significant relationship between type of organization and social area. There is, however, a relationship with size, since significantly more (0·1 per cent level of significance) combined schools tend to be small (up to 99 pupils) and few indeed are larger than two hundred.

We may then begin to examine a little more closely what relationships exist between school organization, school size and the various aspects of the learning and teaching of reading.

READING METHODS

There was no significant difference between the two types of school as to choice of reading method. 'Mixed' methods were equally popular in both types of school. The schools did not differ significantly either in regard to their approach to the teaching of the subject, whether 'child' or 'curriculum' centred, or in the type of considerations which the heads believed most affected their choice of instruction.

When the heads described the ways in which they aroused their pupils' interest in learning to read, significantly more (5 per cent. level) heads of the infant only schools referred to the use of the school library. This is understandable since more infant than combined department schools tended to have an organized library for the specific use of the infants.[1] The schools clearly did not differ in their manner of maintaining pupils' interest in the subject, except in respect to one difference, more infant school heads mentioned the use of home-made books (barely 5 per cent level).

Significantly more (5 per cent level) junior mixed and infant reception class teachers used the single method of look-and-say as an introductory method. Also, they tended to use systematic phonic

[1] This is discussed in some detail in Chapter III and in the relevant section of this chapter.

instruction more, with all or some of their pupils in the reception class, than the infant teachers (5 per cent level). There was no significant difference between the types of school regarding the heads' opinions as to when or if a change of emphasis took place in the teaching of the subject at any stage.

READING MATERIALS AND LIBRARY FACILITIES

There was no significant difference between schools regarding the choice of reading scheme with one exception; more junior mixed and infant schools reported using the Beacon series (5 per cent. level). Also more of these schools tended to make use of more than one scheme in their teaching of the subject (5 per cent level).

The two types of schools differed in their approach to the practice of allowing readers in the scheme to be taken home, more junior mixed and infant head teachers encouraging the practice (5 per cent level) and more reception class teachers in these schools actually allowing it (5 per cent level).

There was no significant difference in relation to the type of reading apparatus used or the purpose for which it was used by the two types of school.

Library facilities were quite another matter; significantly more infant only schools had an organized library (0·1 per cent level) housed in a separate room (1 per cent level) than the junior mixed and infant schools. This difference as we have seen in chapter III is less marked than it seems since a well organized library corner or class library in the smaller combined department schools might well be the equal of the central library of the infant only schools, and adequately fulfil the same function.

Although the types of school had differed in relation to the practice of allowing readers in the basic scheme to be taken home, the groups of schools did not differ significantly regarding whether they allowed library books to be taken home. Where a library was organized, the practice was not common in either type of school.

THE ASSESSMENT OF READING ABILITY

The teachers did not significantly differ regarding their answers describing standards of reading readiness recognized, the proportion of children able to read when they began school, whether or not the reception class teacher tended to aim at a particular standard by the end of the reception class, or in the standard set by the head teacher in terms of 'book criterion'.

Although there was no significant difference in the proportion of head teachers using standardized tests, significantly more (5 per cent level) infant school heads used tests for grading pupils; that is to discover the particularly bright or those below average who would benefit from additional help before promotion to the junior school.

The heads of the two types of school did not differ significantly in their opinion regarding the use of the term 'backward' with infants, both groups showing a similar division of opinion. But of the head teachers who said the term was not applicable to infants, more infant head teachers considered a better term was 'late developer', since it sounded 'less hopeless' than 'backward' which often tended irrevocably to categorize a child (5 per cent level).

The two groups of heads differed most markedly in regard to their provision for backward readers. More infant only head teachers made special provision for these pupils (0·1 per cent level). Only one in four of the junior mixed and infant schools made such provision in comparison with three out of four of the infant schools. Table VI/1 illustrates this point.

TABLE VI/1: *Teachers' Views Regarding the Term 'Backward' and their Provision for Backward Readers in their own Schools—100 Infant Departments/Schools*

SCHOOL ORGANIZATION	TEACHERS BELIEVING TERM APPLICABLE		TOTAL	TEACHERS WHO DID NOT BELIEVE TERM APPLICABLE		TOTAL
	Made Provision	*No Provision*		*Made Provision*	*No Provision*	
Infant	25	7	32	14	7	21
J.M. & I. ..	8	15	23	5	19	24
TOTAL ..	33	22	55	19	26	45

Of those teachers believing the term could be applied to infants, more infant only school heads said they made provision for backward readers (1 per cent level). However, even amongst the heads who did not consider the term applicable to infants there were more heads of infant schools than combined department schools providing help for those pupils needing it. It seems that in the infant only schools,

61

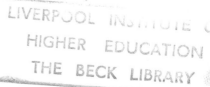

the heads are more conscious of the problem of the children who do not reach the expected standard or maintain the rate of progress of their companions, and this is most probably related to the fact that the children of these schools are transferred to other schools at 7+, thus focussing attention on the progress they have been able to make in the two years spent in the infant school. The junior mixed and infant children stay in the same school, and consequently the age factor assumes less importance, 7+ being less critical.

School Conditions

There was no significant difference between the two groups of schools in respect to the mean age of the school building or the mean material environment score. However, regarding actual facilities and amenities, significantly more infant schools had both stockrooms and cupboards for storage purposes (1 per cent level), more cloakrooms with pegs only (5 per cent level) and had a playground for the use of infants only (1 per cent level).

The teacher-ratio for the two types of school was similar, but the infant schools tended to be larger schools in respect to the number of infants on roll, significantly fewer infant only schools being small or very small schools in size (0·1 per cent level).

The tendency in the junior mixed and infant schools seemed to be for slightly fewer married teachers to be employed than single teachers, but the difference did not reach significance. During the field work when the writer visited many of the schools, heads of some of the junior mixed and infant schools mentioned the problems of employing married teachers. In these smaller schools, it was often difficult to arrange for a married teacher's class to be taken by other members of staff if she was forced by a family crisis to be absent or late. The heads of the combined department schools are aware of this problem and prepared to cope with the difficulties which may arise, because they are appreciative of the understanding and experience the married teacher, with children of her own, can bring to the task of teaching infants.

There was no significant difference between the groups in respect to the age distribution amongst staff, their training and experience, or the training and experience of the reception class teacher.

There was no information available to distinguish the heads of the two types of school in terms of specific training for infant school work. However, any difference in the training or experience of these two groups of heads was likely to be chiefly a sex difference.

READING ATTAINMENT

The reading attainment of the pupils in these two types of school did not differ significantly at the end of the infant course, either on the basis of the results of a group test of reading attainment or the teachers' estimates of achievement using the 'book criterion'. Tables VI/2 and VI/3 illustrate this point.

TABLE VI/2: *Mean Test Scores for Infant Only and Junior Mixed and Infant Schools—65 Infant Departments/Schools*

ORGANIZATION	MEAN SCORE	STANDARD ERROR	NUMBER OF CHILDREN
Infant only	10·84	0·19	2,006
Junior Mixed and Infant	11·30	0·26	1,116
TOTAL	11·00	0·15	3,122

TABLE VI/3: *Percentage Distribution of Pupils for Each Book Level— 63[1] Infant Departments/Schools*

BOOK LEVEL	TYPE OF ORGANIZATION				OVERALL
	Infant		J.M. & I.		
	%	N	%	N	%
Book 4 and above	40·8	821	40·9	486	40·9
Book 2 and 3	42·4	855	43·2	512	42·7
Book 1 and below ..	16·8	337	15·9	188	16·4
TOTAL	100·0	2013	100·0	1186	100·0

Thus there is no evidence from these results to suggest that at the end of the infant school stage, one type of organization produces better results than the other.

[1] There were two schools, one infant and one junior mixed and infant, who did not complete the individual pupils' book level assessments, although they carried out the testing programme.

CONCLUSION

It is apparent from a review of the findings of the initial survey and the reading attainment of the pupils in these schools, that school organization had relatively little effect upon either the practice and conditions of teaching reading or the level of reading attainment. Apart from the basic difference of size, the number of infants on roll, the schools differed only in three major ways: in the existence and the use made of an organized library for the sole use of the infant age range of children, in their provision for backward readers, and certain physical conditions primarily involving space evidenced by the difference in storage facilities and playing areas. In the light of these findings the close similarity of standards of reading attainment in the two types of school is consistent with the homogeneity of approach and method reported.

CHAPTER VII

Social Area

THE association between the environment from which a school draws its pupils and reading attainment is well known as is the closely similar relation between environment and intelligence. The complex relationship between intelligence, school attainment and environment is examined in much greater length in a second report[1] dealing with this London inquiry. For the purpose of the present study, the school environment was classified on the basis of the distribution of social groups within the area in which the school was situated. It is suggested that in areas of predominantly semi-skilled and unskilled occupations, reading will not be a highly valued skill and that in consequence children from such areas will be comparatively less motivated to acquire the skill. The actual method of classifying schools is described in detail in the second report, but it is sufficient here to say that on the basis of occupational distribution, it was possible to place the schools in three different groups, which were summarized as (1) Lower Working Class (2) Working Class and (3) Middle Class. The main distinguishing characteristics of the three types of school are now described in more detail.

Social Area 1: This area was densely residential, but at the same time it included mixed industrial and dockside activities. Some of the area had been re-developed since the war when it was extensively damaged, but at the time of the survey parts were still awaiting reconstruction and tended to show many of the signs of economic stagnation—a 'depressed area'. Occupations were usually semi-skilled or unskilled. The schools in these areas encountered m any of the problems found in the inner older areas of development of urban communities[2]. Their pupils came from economically and culturally disadvantaged homes, and their attitudes towards the value and function of education

---

[1] GOODACRE, E. J. (1967), op. cit.

[2] See volume of related studies: PASSOW, H. A., ed. (1963). *Education in Depressed Areas.* New York: Bureau of Publications, Teachers' College, Columbia University.

were quite different from those of the pupils in the other areas. Such children appear to have little preparation, either for recognizing the importance of education as a means of acquiring other skills more highly valued by society, or for being able to cope with the kinds of thinking and learning which the school tends to expect of them.

Social Area 2: Having markedly less non-residential property than the previous area, this is not an industrial and commercial area but almost solely residential development at high density. In the middle of the last century, a great many of its substantial buildings were sub-divided and converted into additional accommodation. It differed from the previous area in that occupations tended to be predominantly skilled and semi-skilled, and there was no abnormally high percentage of occupied males in the lowest social class as was found in social area 1. It is a working class area with some of its residents ambitious to move out of its drab overcrowded housing conditions to the more truly surburban areas of the outer development of the Authority.

Social Area 3: This third group of schools is a composite one in that most of the schools were situated in the outer ring of urban development, but some schools were in the older, more central area of the 'city' where residential and non-residential buildings existed together. The latter area is one where in the past and still to-day the older residential property is not retained for dwelling but is taken over for use as shops and offices. The two areas have similar distributions of occupations though, with larger proportions from the higher social class groups. In comparison with the other two groups of schools from area 1 and 2, the social area 3 schools can be described as predominantly middle class and 'white collar', although in the central area there were two schools situated in 'pockets' of slum housing. The majority of these pupils came from homes where there was belief in and support of formal schooling, and its value as a means of achieving upward mobility.

In this chapter, the material collected in the survey has been examined for the effects of differences in social area from which pupils come—that is, whether the schools of differing social background facing different problems tended to adopt different methods and practices as a result of the difficulties they encountered.

READING METHODS

There was no significant difference between the schools in the different social areas in relation to their choice of method or approach, but in describing the considerations which affected the type of instruction used, significantly more heads in the lower working class area, than in either the working or middle class areas mentioned the factor of pupils' home background (5 per cent level).

In describing the ways in which they sought to arouse pupils' interest in learning to read, significantly fewer head teachers in the middle class areas referred to the use of wall stories (5 per cent level). It may be remembered that this method relies upon the sentence as the meaningful unit, and is probably of particular appeal to children from social environments in which hard covered books are comparatively unfamiliar in comparison with the visual communication of television or film.

There was no significant difference between the groups of schools regarding the choice of introductory method, or whether systematic phonic instruction was given to the reception class pupils. In each social area, there was a similar proportion of reception class teachers who were in the habit of giving phonic instruction to all their five-year-olds, irrespective of the background, experience or mental ability of their pupils. Heads in the different social areas did not differ significantly in their replies regarding a change of emphasis in the infant school or the general stage at which systematic phonic instruction tended to be introduced.

READING MATERIALS AND LIBRARY FACILITIES

Social area appeared not to influence the choice of reading scheme, and 'Janet and John' with its middle class characters and somewhat indefinite background was equally popular in schools in all areas. In only seven schools was a reading scheme not in operation in the reception class, and these schools were distributed throughout the three social areas as follows: two in the lower working class area, one in a working class area, and four in the middle class areas. There were some differences observable in regard to the practice of allowing pupils to take home the readers in the series. The replies of the head and reception class teachers in the lower working class areas suggest that more heads than reception class teachers answered with an unqualified 'yes' (1 per cent). When, however, all affirmative answers, irrespective of qualification, are considered the results are non-significant. It seems that although the heads of lower working class schools say they encourage pupils to take home their readers, in actual practice the reception class teacher may not allow all their pupils to do so. There may be several reasons for this: a fear that books will be lost or damaged; that pupils' parents are unable to give any assistance or 'hear' children effectively; or because these pupils are not considered old enough or capable of benefiting from this practice. The attitude of the class teacher seemed to be unaffected by the school social area, and possibly different reasons prompt similar decisions. Indeed the analysis undertaken for the second report[1] suggests that the practice of allowing readers to be taken home by pupils is related to the teacher's own social background. Working class teachers expect and probably encourage parents to borrow the books, whereas teachers of middle class origin expect parents to buy the reader as a means of showing their interest in their children's progress.

The schools in the three social areas did not differ significantly in respect to their use of reading apparatus (either type or purpose), or the existence or use of organized libraries.

ASSESSMENT OF READING ABILITY

No significant differences were observable regarding the groups' standards of reading readiness of the proportion of children able to read at entry.

There was, somewhat surprisingly, no significant differences between the groups of schools in respect to the heads' estimates of book levels achieved by the end of the infant course. In fact, the teachers of schools in the lower working class areas tended to estimate a smaller proportion of pupils on or below book one, than the teachers in the other two areas, but the difference was not significant. Table VII/1 shows the proportions, if the older city schools are removed from the less homogeneous middle class group of schools, and only the suburban and outer urban development schools considered. The trend regarding poor readers is less evident then than on the previous analysis, and the proportions of good readers increased the higher the social area, although the difference is still not significant.

There was no significant difference between the groups of schools in relation to the use of standardized tests, or in the teachers'

[1] GOODACRE, E. J., *op. cit.*

68

TABLE VII/1: *Predicted Percentage of Pupils Attaining Each Book Level by End of Infant Schooling—100 Infant Departments/Schools*

BOOK LEVEL	SOCIAL AREAS				TOTAL
	1 (N=38) *Schools*	*2* (N=30) *Schools*	*3* (N=32) *Schools*	*3 Omitting 6 City Schools*	
Book 4+	52	53	52	58	52
Books 2–3	38	34	33	29	36
Book 1 and below ..	10	13	15	13	12

opinions regarding the application of the term 'backward' or their provision for such children. In the lower working class area, 58 per cent of head teachers considered the term could be applied, 53 per cent in the working and middle class areas. Provision for backward readers tended to be provided in a larger proportion of schools, the higher the social area (47 per cent; 53 per cent; 56 per cent respectively) but the differences again were too small to be significant. The pressure accorded by the two-year time limitation, which the infant only schools felt, appeared to influence head teachers' practice in this regard more than any attitudes based on a desire to compensate such children for deficiencies within their background, or ameliorative efforts designed to counteract the accumulative effects of the inter-action of poor environment, low motivation and the level of in-herited ability.

SCHOOL CONDITIONS

The groups of schools did not differ significantly either in the mean age of school buildings or the mean material environment score, although there was significant difference in the variances between social areas. This result was somewhat unexpected in view of the association reported in the Kent study by Morris, although a study by Halsey[1] in S. W. Hertfordshire schools suggested that the relation-ship between economic status of school population and material environment was a loose one (correlation $\pm$ 0·202), and Halsey

---

[1] HALSEY, A. H. (1955). 'The relation between education and social inability with particular reference to the Grammar School since 1944'. Ph.D. thesis, London University.

believed the results would have been similar to the earlier findings by Glass[1] if the most recent schools had been omitted from the total sample of Hertfordshire schools studies. Ruth Glass had found in Middlesborough an extremely close relationship. Kemp also working in a group of London schools, found no significant relationship between the variables' scores for school building and socio-economic status. The difference between the London studies and those in other counties may result from the fact that London, particularly the lower working class areas, experienced severe war damage as a consequence of which, a large amount of the new school building has taken place in these areas and the older areas no longer have a high proportion of old, out-dated schools.

The schools in the different areas did not differ significantly regarding amenities and facilities, but fewer lower working class head teachers and more middle class head teachers believed their schools were well located (1 per cent level) and attractive (5 per cent level). Qualified answers were excluded from these two tests.

There was a tendency observed for more of the schools in the middle class areas to be very small, and fewer to be moderate or small in size, in contrast with the schools in the lower working class area, fewer of which were very small and some moderately small (5 per cent level). The difference in size was not highly significant.

The pupil/teacher ratio tended to be more favourable the higher the social area (5 per cent level). The difference was not significant between the two working class areas, but between the two extremes, the difference was at the 5 per cent level and between the working and middle class area schools at one per cent. It should be mentioned that the middle class schools included two new schools whose numbers were not complete at the time of the survey and may partly explain the comparatively better teacher/ratio of the middle class group of schools, although a greater shortage of teachers could be expected in the working class areas in comparison with 'suburban' Social Area 3 since more teachers were likely to live in the middle class areas and the home counties.

The impression had been gained during the field work that the lower working class schools might have a larger proportion of very young teachers and single teachers, since in the other two areas, there would be more competition for posts, married teachers particularly, seeking jobs near their own homes in the 'better' residential areas.

[1] GLASS, R. (1948). *The Social Background of a Plan—A Study of Middlesbrough.* London: Routledge & Kegan Paul.

The lower working class area did have a larger proportion of young teachers, whilst the working class areas had the highest proportion of teachers over forty years. The lowest proportion of married teachers occurred in the lower working class area, but in neither case (marital status or age distribution) did the difference reach significance.

A slightly larger proportion of the teachers in the lower working class areas, tended to be those without training for infant teaching, and the highest proportion of teachers in their first year of training was found in this same area. The differences again are not significant, and in any case the number of teachers in the total sample without training or experience is small. Even so, it does seem unfortunate that a higher proportion of such teachers should be working with those children in particular need of confident, accurate and stimulating teaching. That this occurs is almost certainly due to the tendency for there to be greater competition for posts in the 'better' areas and the reputation of lower working class schools for offering unattractive conditions, sordid, depressing locations, and long journeys to and from schools for teachers, conditions which seem to outweigh the actual amenities and facilities existing in such schools.

Of the nine schools where the reception class was being taken by a teacher in her first year of teaching, five were in the lower working class areas, three in the working class, and one in the middle class. The difference is not significant, but the proportions may tend to reflect the difficulty which faces heads particularly in the lower working class areas, where the majority of the staff may be young and comparatively inexperienced. For instance in two schools in lower working class areas, the head teachers had little choice, since in both the staff consisted of five members all under twenty-five years of age. In such staffs, marriage can claim high proportions and result in unstable staffing conditions, and several heads complained of young teachers, who disappeared to the altar just as they were becoming assets.

The small proportion of reception class teachers in the middle class area with nursery experience is probably related to the fact that there tend to be fewer nursery schools and classes in these areas.

READING ATTAINMENT

Although the schools did not differ significantly in their approach to the teaching of reading in their materials and methods, their estimates of readiness and their expectations regarding standards, and their material and staffing conditions, there were significant differences between the groups of schools in the pupils' reading attainment at the end of the infant course. These differences (Tables VII/2 and 3) were shown both in reading test scores and in the 'book criterion'.

The lower working class schools were markedly inferior to the rest. There were less significant differences between the working and middle class schools.

Table VII/2 shows the mean raw scores for the London children on the National Survey (1960) attainment group test, and the mean attainment of pupils by the three broad social areas. The mean raw scores are given also for the sub-divisions within these social areas, which correspond with differences in social class distribution and to some extent developmental and topographical conditions.

The Social Class Indices and geographical locations of these sub-divisions are as follows:

Lower Working Class:	1. Eastern	161.2
	2. Southern	163.6
Working Class:	1. Western	174.0
	2. South-Eastern	174.2
	3. Northern	176.5
Middle Class:	1. City—Central	180.7
	2. City—Western	196.6
	3. Suburban—South Eastern	182.4
	4. Suburban—South Western	188.8

TABLE VII/2: *Mean Test Scores for Pupils in Schools in Different Social Areas—65 Infant Departments/Schools*

SOCIAL AREA	SUB-DIVISIONS	MEAN	STANDARD ERROR	MEAN THREE AREAS		N
				Mean	*S.E.*	
1 Lower Working Class	1	8·97	0·32	9·39	0·24	598
	2	9·84	0·35			568
2 Working Class	1	10·78	0·41	12·08	0·25	361
	2	12·33	0·36			552
	3	13·84	0·68			153
3 Middle Class	1 2 } City	9·96 } 8·53 }	0·76 } 2·20 }	9·75 } 11·89	0·31	99 17
	3 4 } Suburban	11·43 } 14·72 }	0·38 } 0·71 }	12·21 }		590 184
TOTAL	—	—	—	11·00	0·15	3,122

Taken as a whole the differences between the set of nine sub-divisions of social area means are significant at 0·1 per cent level. When the three main social area means are considered, the difference is significant at 0·1 per cent with the somewhat unexpected result that the pupils in working class area schools show superior attainment. However, it will be recalled that the middle class grouping is a composite one, and if only the results of the suburban schools are considered—that is, the older, inner city schools omitted—then the superiority of the working class schools disappears. The difference between the city and suburban middle class schools is significantly (1 per cent) in favour of the suburban schools. Similarly the differences between the means of the sub-divisions within the working class area are significant at the same level. However, the difference between the means of the two sub-divisions in the lower working class area—the areas either side of the river in the older, depressed areas—is not significant.

TABLE VII/3: *Pupils' Achieved Book Levels in Different Social Area Schools—63 Infant Departments/Schools*

BOOK LEVELS	SOCIAL AREAS										OVER-ALL %
	1. Lower Working Class		2. Working Class		3. Middle Class						
					City Schools Only		Suburban Schools Only		All Middle Class Schools		
	%	N	%	N	%	N	%	N	%	N	
Book 4 and above	35·1	430	42·7	451	33·9	41	48·4	385	46·5	426	40·9
Book 2 and 3	49·0	601	42·1	445	44·6	54	33·5	267	35·0	321	42·7
Book 1 and below	15·9	194	15·2	161	21·5	26	18·1	144	18·5	170	16·4
TOTAL	100·0	1225	100·0	1057	100·0	121	100·0	796	100·0	917	100·0

Table VII/3 shows the proportion of pupils in the different groups of schools estimated by their teachers to have reached the various book levels by the end of the infant course. The difference between the two working class groups was highly significant (0·1 per cent) with more working class pupils being on book 4 or beyond. The difference between the middle and working class schools was significant, but less so (1 per cent). Indeed when the city schools were omitted from the middle class grouping, the difference between middle and working class schools was at the 5 per cent level. More pupils in the suburban, middle class schools were estimated by their teachers to be reading book 4 or beyond; but also these schools had a larger proportion of pupils estimated to be reading book 1 and below, i.e. 'poor readers' by their teachers' standards. The difference between the city and suburban middle class schools was significant at the 5 per cent level, more children from suburban schools being in the highest category—that is, the difference between the two types of middle class schools which made up this composite grouping, was not as significant as that between the two working class groups of schools.

To summarize these results, the working class pupils appeared to do better than might have been predicted, especially in relation to tested attainment. They were superior to the middle class pupils, although this advantage disappeared if the middle class city schools were excluded from the latter grouping. In relation to the teachers' estimates of pupils' attainment on the basis of 'book criterion', the middle class pupils were superior to the working class pupils but with the omission of the city schools, the difference was less significant. The lower working class pupils, however, were markedly inferior in comparison with the other two groups, in relation to both tested and estimated attainment.

Conclusion

It is apparent from this summary of the teachers' replies to the initial questionnaire and their pupils' reading attainment, whether on test scores or estimated levels, that although the social area of the school had little effect upon teaching methods, materials, standards or even school conditions, there is a relationship between social area and reading attainment, which becomes more marked the lower the social area.

In only two ways did the schools in the different areas differ noticeably regarding practice and conditions. These were the heads' encouragement of the custom of allowing readers to be taken home by pupils, a practice which may be related to the teacher's social class origin, and in the head's opinion about the suitability of the location of their school. The superiority of the working and middle class schools in comparison with the lower working class pupil is marked. The most interesting aspect of these results is the fact that the working class schools' attainment is not, as might have been expected, significantly different from that of the middle class schools, in relation to tested attainment, but the expected superiority of the latter schools is apparent when the measure is the teachers' assessments. The working class schools did not appear to differ appreciably either in practice, methods or conditions from the other area schools. Some aspects of this phenomenon are discussed in the concluding chapter and certain suggestions outlined, which may provide a partial explanation of the comparative superiority of the working class pupils in relation to tested but not assessed reading attainment.

CHAPTER VIII

Summary and Conclusions

THE findings reported here are the first results of a three year programme of research into the problems of teaching beginners to read, and the main aim of this present survey is to provide a picture of the infant schools' methods of teaching reading, the schemes, materials and practices used, and how, if at all, the two important factors of school organization and social area affect this. These broad factors are studied in relation to the final reading attainment of the pupils.

We may now examine the results first in terms of the practice of the infant school by comparison with those of the Junior school about which evidence was obtained in the earlier Kent inquiry. We may then examine the importance of the two variables, school organization and social area, particularly in the light of how schools might have varied their practice to meet the problems which appear to face them, especially those arising from the social background of their pupils.

THE FINDINGS IN RELATION TO THE KENT INQUIRY

Reading methods

The Kent inquiry demonstrated the importance attached by junior school teachers to the use of 'mixed' methods in the teaching of reading. The picture in the infant school appears to be similar. The majority of teachers use all the main methods of teaching reading, and tend to differ principally in the order in which they introduce the basic methods and the importance they attach to any aspect at different stages of children's development.

When the type of approach used is distinguished as being either 'child centred' or 'curriculum centred', there appears to be some evidence that during the past five years there may have been a change in infant teachers' opinions and practices. The importance of the basic skills and the value of a controlled and planned classroom environment received more emphasis in these London schools than the individual freedom of the child and the merits of activity methods which were popular among Kent teachers, and this possibly reflects the pendulum swing of opinion. It is of interest to note, since such a climate of opinion may be more favourable towards other changes in educational method. For instance, the recent interest in the units and stages of learning involved in the development of the total skill is related probably to the introduction and use of teaching machines. The simplification of early reading tasks, such as that provided by the use of materials printed in the augmented roman alphabet, may have a special appeal to teachers after a period when analytic methods attracted much attention. These latter types of reading methods, with their smaller emphasis upon systematic instruction and their avowed aim to develop reading for meaning rather than mere word recognition, are more difficult to test. Thus, in the early stages at all events concrete results are hard to come by, and the teacher has less satisfactory evidence of successful teaching. It may well be that synthetic methods, because they are dogmatic, tend to lessen teachers' anxieties and provide an emotional satisfaction. As yet there has been no research designed solely to study types of reading methods in relation to the personal satisfaction and security which they provide to the teacher.

Certainly, if teachers are showing less interest in the motivations of learning to read and rather more in the nature and operation of the skill, this was to be expected since probably sufficient emphasis had been laid upon the importance of the learner's motivation, and what is needed is a reappraisal of the knowledge which exists about the elements which constitute the total skill. This would involve the definition and simplification of those reading tasks which comprise learning to read, and this would increase our knowledge and awareness of the successive stages and developmental nature of the operation. The emphasis would then increasingly be upon the appropriateness of each task to the observed level of motivation.

A change in the climate of opinion is perhaps indicated also in the comparison of Kent and London teachers' answers concerning the major considerations which affected the type of instruction given. The ability and professional skills of teachers, in particular their knowledge and experience of the stages in the teaching of the subject, increase in importance when the curriculum itself is of high significance. Fewer London heads mentioned the needs of individual children as a major consideration, nor did they make much of the size of classes; the relative sizes of the classes in the Kent and London studies were not established in fact. The size of the class assumes less importance, if one's approach is not predominantly 'child centred' with its emphasis upon individual rather than group or class instruction.

If these differences represent a swing of opinion towards more formal approaches, one might expect there to be a corresponding increase in the use of systematic phonic instruction with five-year-olds, and that the choice of introductory method would be synthetic rather than analytic.   Certainly there is evidence from the London teachers that a larger proportion of teachers were giving all pupils systematic phonic instruction earlier; and that if we take account of the slight difference in the wording of the question to the London teachers, more were using combinations of methods, including phonics, in their introductory work than in Kent.   Despite the view that an early introduction to sounds may affect later fluency and comprehension, and that a minimum mental age of 7+ is necessary for the comprehension of phonic elements, two out of every five infant teachers in London were giving systematic phonic instruction to *all* their pupils, irrespective of either the individual child's mental maturity or home background.   A later stage of the research programme will provide information, not so much to determine whether these teachers were right or wrong, but whether early systematic reading instruction has different results in terms of the particular social environment of the schools.

Reading materials and library facilities

Five years had elapsed between the carrying out of the Kent inquiry and the London survey.   It may be that this lapse of time is alone the reason for the extremely rapid increase in the popularity of a particular reading series, 'Janet and John'.   This series was reported as being in use in more than half the London schools in comparison with one in five of those in Kent.   The scheme had come on the market only three years before the Kent inquiry and, from the answers of the teachers at that time, an increase in the use of the scheme could have been anticipated, in the same way that there were suggestions in discussions with the teachers during the London inquiry that the McKee reading scheme was gaining ground. Another fact that should be remembered is that the design of the 'Janet and John' scheme provides for the choice of a phonic or whole-word approach, so that the scheme has an appeal to a larger group of teachers than one based on a single approach.

However, the immense popularity of a single series is worthy of comment.   Only 18 per cent of the London infant schools were using two or more schemes.   The reading scheme or series with its set of readers of increasing difficulty, appears to be of immense help to teachers and to provide a source of security, especially to infant teachers straight from college. These appeared to find the manual of instruction and the controlled vocabulary of particular help, since some of these young teachers reported that they had had only limited instruction in the actual mechanics of teaching reading in their training colleges; although most had no complaints about the opportunity their lecturers had provided for looking at different reading schemes and materials.

It can be argued also that the use of one particular scheme in so many schools may be of considerable benefit when more and more children change from school to school because their families move. The introductory book of this series is centred on two children, presented as predominantly middle class stereotypes. The appeal of this to children of vastly different social backgrounds, is questionable; the writer recalls the disgusted comment of a lower working class five-year-old, who summed up John as 'soppy' and refused to show any interest in his exploits.

The popularity of a single scheme and the fact that only nine London schools did not use a basic scheme in the reception class, supports the view that teachers' opinions have somewhat changed since the Kent inquiry. Increasingly, emphasis is being placed on the value of the reading scheme itself as a form of curriculum, by publishers in particular. It was therefore not unexpected to find that the infant schools were making considerable use of reading apparatus, but it is important to note that both the published and the teacher-made type were in use, and that only a small proportion of schools was using such apparatus for class purposes only.

Undoubtedly this type of material plays an important part in teaching beginners, providing opportunities for practice and enabling repetitive learning to be more enjoyable. Since reading apparatus was being used so widely in the infant school, the reluctance of junior teachers to utilize such teaching aids reported in the Kent inquiry assumes even more importance. Over half the junior schools in the Kent inquiry did not use reading apparatus at all, since they considered that children over seven regarded such material as 'babyish' and, therefore, tended to derive little benefit from it. Obviously such material must have infant school connotations for junior pupils, but it is difficult to justify the exclusion of aids found of such value to the infant learner for this reason alone—especially when one considers the low reading standards of some children in the first year junior classes.

The present survey showed that the infant only schools had taken every opportunity to establish libraries for their pupils' use and that often an immense amount of thought and imagination had gone into the setting up of these collections. In comparison with Kent, these urban schools, especially the infant only ones, were infinitely better placed regarding library facilities. Undoubtedly the efforts by publishers over the last five years to provide reading material suitable for infants have contributed to the generally high standard of library facilities available in infant schools. Although it must be added that the view expressed by teachers in the Kent inquiry, that the material available for lower juniors was too limited, received support from the teachers of the older infants in the London survey. There is still a need at this stage for additional material if publishers could supply it.

Assessment of reading ability

It was suggested by the Consultative Committee on the Primary School (Board of Education, 1931, reprinted 1952) that the task of the junior school teacher was predominantly that of developing reading comprehension, since only a few 'backward' children would be in need of systematic instruction in reading mechanics after the age of seven. In fact the Kent inquiry reported that approximately 45 per cent of the children entering the junior school were still in need of the kind of teaching associated with the infant school. In the London survey it was noticeable that infant teachers, especially those in the infant only type of school, experienced anxiety in respect to the standards expected of their pupils by the end of their schooling. It is hoped that findings such as those of the Kent inquiry may to some extent alleviate this. Certainly, the unrealistic approach of some educationists towards the problems of teaching infants, permitted assumptions such as that quoted regarding the main function of the junior teacher. The wide range of abilities of children, the varying effect of home background on motivation to read, and the varying length of time spent by pupils in the infant school, must set limitations upon the achievement which can be attained by the majority of pupils by the end of the infant school course. The London infant teachers, estimating the levels of attainment possible by the time of transfer, suggested proportions of good and poor readers similar to those actually found in the Kent inquiry at the beginning of the junior school course. Since the standards attained in Kent by the end of the primary course were above the average for the country as a whole, the London teachers were generally setting themselves fairly high standards. The infant teachers were only too well aware of factors which could affect the standards they hoped to attain, and it is one of the aims of the further stages of the research, to examine the effect of teachers' aspirations for their pupils on their achieved level of attainment, especially within the different social areas.

The needs of children of below average intelligence, handicapped by unfavourable circumstances, was a major problem of teachers in the junior school, and a number of the Kent teachers considered the best method of dealing with this was to secure the services of an experienced teacher, who could remain unattached to a class and provide individual help, although in fact this solution was rarely possible at the time of the Kent inquiry. The present survey found these infant schools were, for certain reasons, more favourably placed in regard to having additional assistance, which was used to help pupils making inadequate progress. It was very noticeable that, although both types of infant school were divided as to the applicability of the term backward to infant children, significantly more infant only schools made every effort to make special provision for those pupils in need of additional help, whether they might be described as 'backward', 'slow' or 'late developers'. This appears to be clear evidence of the anxiety felt by the teachers in the separate department schools at the prospect of their pupils' transfer at seven.

Despite the problem of the backward reader, the Kent inquiries found that junior teachers made relatively little use of diagnostic tests. The London infant teachers were asked about their use of standardized reading tests, and almost twice as many schools were found to be using standardized tests as in Kent. This seems more likely to be a reflection of the increasing acceptance of the reliability and value of this form of measurement to the teacher than a difference in practice between the two types of primary education.

The training and experience of the reception class teacher

An important finding of the Kent investigation was the need for junior teachers, especially those of the transition class to possess a knowledge of infant methods and experience of teaching reading from the early stages. We were interested to know whether the staffing of the reception class in the infant school presented similar difficulties. The findings seem to suggest that, although there are certain problems, the situation is not comparable. Since few nursery classes exist, it is not surprising that few reception class teachers have experience of these classes. It is unfortunate that, at the present

81

time, there seems little prospect of any large-scale introduction of nursery classes; new entrants to infant teaching might benefit considerably from working with such classes.

SCHOOL ORGANIZATION AND SOCIAL AREA

The importance of school organization appears to be closely related to the factor of size, and in Chapter VI it was concluded that the type of organization mainly affected conditions related to size, such as the use of space, the existence of an infant library, storage facilities, and provision for backward readers which is related to the use of additional staff, as well as the pressure exerted by the transfer at seven. Certainly in this research, organization appeared to be unrelated to the level of reading attainment, nor did it have any appreciable effect upon the choice of methods or materials.

The Kent inquiry showed that schools of differing social background were faced with very different problems in the teaching of reading, and having estimated the possibility of the effects of school organization, we shall now turn to the other aim of this research: how do the schools in the different social areas tend to differ in regard to conditions of learning and practice, and the extent to which they adapt their methods and materials as a consequence.

The most important finding of this survey amongst urban infant schools is that broadly speaking the social area of the school had little effect upon teaching methods, materials, standards or even school conditions.

'Mixed' methods were those most often reported, irrespective of the social area of the school. Even the whole-word approach often described as suitable for use with duller children, was found to be no more popular in the lower working class area than either of the other two areas, despite the fact that significantly more of the teachers in schools in the former areas believed that their pupils were only of average or below average intelligence. Even when the controversial question of the use of phonics in the reception class was studied, the social area of the school made no appreciable difference in regard to this practice. In each social area, a similar proportion of teachers believed the practice to be effective.

It has already been mentioned that one reading scheme was particularly popular in all areas, irrespective of the pupils' social background and the environmental experiences which they might bring to the reading situation.

Although teachers tended to differ in the type of approach they adopted to the teaching of reading, being either predominantly child or curriculum centred in the approach they used, neither type of approach was found to be more favoured by the teachers in one area rather than another.

Asked about the major considerations affecting their choice of instructions, a quarter of the head teachers claimed that the particular social background of the pupils they taught was an important aspect, whilst a third considered the needs of individual children were the determining factor. In view of these opinions, it would not have been unexpected to find an association between the use of particular methods and certain areas, at least in regard to the choice of commencing method, if not a single basic method. Similarly, one might have expected to find more schools using more than one basic scheme and a greater variety in the choice of scheme. However, it appears that in most cases, the needs of individual children and groups of children of varying degrees of motivation to acquire the skill, are considered by these teachers to be met by the provision of a variety of supplementary reading material and the use of different types of reading apparatus rather than by the adaptation of either scheme or approach to the problems and difficulties presented by particular environmental conditions.

The lower working class areas are those in which social conditions are such as to be least likely to encourage children to want or need to learn to read. It may be that almost exclusive reliance upon the provision of variety and quantity of reading materials, is insufficient to arouse the interest to learn to read of these children, if neither method, reading scheme nor approach are adapted to their background experience and the values engendered by it. This is one of the questions which a subsequent report will consider in detail—whether significantly good or poor levels of reading attainment within particular social areas are associated with differences in method, scheme or approach, and whether it is possible to produce conclusive evidence as to the effectiveness of different methods and practice in the teaching of reading in areas of high or low motivation to acquire the skill.

Factors in the learning situation

The relationship of reading methods and children's social background has received scant attention hitherto in research into the teaching of reading. The exponents of the synthetic and analytic methods have put forward their claims for success, but the effectiveness of particular types of methods with children of different experiential backgrounds has scarcely been explored. In learning to read there are four very important factors:

(a) the time at which systematic instruction is introduced;
(b) the form this instruction takes;
(c) the previous experience of the child, including his motivation and his grasp of languages;
(d) the experience, confidence and background of the teacher.

The stage at which systematic instruction can be introduced can be lowered if the reading task is simplified. The research to date seems to show that early systematic phonic instruction can produce favourable results, but since synthetic methods tend to depend largely on associative types of learning, this initial advantage may not be maintained, especially towards the end of the junior schooling where reading becomes a means of acquiring and using information— a communicative process and not merely word recognition.

In comparison, analytic methods, although possibly slower in obtaining results, produce reading for meaning and a more fundamental grasp of the skill. Also, analytic methods demand considerable opportunities and experiences in order to formulate the basic reading concepts underlying this type of learning pattern. Such opportunities and experience may have been provided by the child's social background. Where this is not so, the teacher may have to supply them and the rate of progress of these disadvantaged pupils is slower as a consequence.

Language patterns and reading methods

The social areas differ in regard to the factor of motivation, but of equal importance is the form of language used in the social environment. Papers[1] by Bernstein have suggested that the working class pupils are users of a 'public' language, and experience difficulty in making generalizations and in concept formation, far more so than middle class pupils, whose language pattern is such as to enable them to extend their experience and knowledge by the elaboration of experience and the building up of new concepts. If this is so, it is possible that teachers in lower and working class area schools are setting themselves an extremely difficult task in teaching reading by analytic methods, since they are attempting to change their pupils' language pattern, and not merely to arouse a feeble motivation.

[1] BERNSTEIN, B. (1961). *Educational Research*, Vol. III, No. 3, pp. 163-76.

Such teachers may ultimately succeed, but the rate at which the skill develops may be slow in comparison with users of synthetic methods, and never equal that established by teachers, whose pupils have both the necessary motivation and the desirable experiences inculcated long before they reach the classroom. In comparison, teachers who use synthetic methods with working class pupils are using methods which fit in with the existing language pattern. Drill and repetition play an important part, and within the common language system, reiteration of words and phrases is a characteristic of the 'public' language. However, difficulties probably first arise with the introduction of the exceptions to the rules, and neither the language system nor the type of reading instruction produce the necessary flexibility of mind to grasp and use these exceptions. Reading for meaning can supply the ability to read the exception, the general sense supplying clues, but since synthetic methods tend to encourage a facility in word recognition rather than comprehension, this is the stage at which the initial advantage may be lost, unless the home and social background has supplied the motivation to carry the child past this learning plateau.

Teachers and their reading methods and expectations

So far the discussion has been concerned primarily with the basic teaching methods in relation to differences in the experiential background of the beginner. But one must not lose sight of the teacher. Her values, attitudes and expectations are of equal importance, and are probably intimately related to her own social class origin. For instance, it is quite possible that the teacher of working class origin may be more emotionally secure when using synthetic rather than analytic reading methods, but this does not presume that such methods will automatically produce success, if both teacher and pupils are of working class origin. It may well be that the working class teacher's expectations of working class pupils are lower than those of a middle class teacher, as the former is over critical and underestimates the potential ability of her pupils in order to emphasize her own social mobility and attained social status, as evidenced by gaining entry to the teaching profession.

As yet there is little evidence regarding the effect of teachers' social class origin on their attitudes and estimation of their pupils' abilities, potential and achieved. But it is possible that such a factor is operating in relation to the tested and estimated reading attainment of the pupils in the London survey, and that the explantaion for the similar reading achievement of the working and middle class area schools, in comparison with the significantly lower attainment of the lower working class children, is that the working class teachers in the lower working class area schools, by reason of their status anxiety, under-estimate these pupils' ability as do the teachers of middle class origin in the same area, who do so because they are unfamiliar with such children and their level of achievement. Whereas the teachers in the middle class area, irrespective of social class origin, tend to over-estimate the ability of their pupils and depress the level of achieved attainment, possibly by reason of setting too high standards, which produce too great a level of anxiety in the pupils or dissipate their interest.

The working class area teachers probably have the most realistic view of the situation, tending neither to over- or under-estimate, and as a consequence their pupils' attainment equals that of the middle class pupils of whom possibly an unrealistic standard is demanded. For instance, the estimated proportions of 'poor' or 'backward' readers were similar throughout the three social areas, despite the fact that the lower working class teachers considered they had more children of average and below average intelligence. The trend, although not significant, was for more middle class area schools to make provision for such readers, whether they agreed with the term or not, than the schools in the lower working class area. The implication is that the teachers expect a higher standard from all children of 'better' homes, whereas a proportion of backward readers is considered to be inevitable in the lower social class areas. This attitude was implicit in the two characteristic types of statement which the writer heard from teachers whilst visiting the schools in the different areas during the field work. Often in referring to the work of individual pupils, a teacher would comment: 'She should be able to do better, she comes from a good home', or conversely, 'What can you expect, he comes from a poor home'. This question of what teachers really mean by the use of the terms 'good' and 'poor' home background is treated at some length in the second report of the research, and has already been the subject of an article in *Educational Research*[1].

Future research

In view of the factors just discussed, it is intended that the two future reports of the London inquiry shall have as their subjects two distinct but related aspects of the teaching of beginners: (1) an

[1] GOODACRE, E. J. (1961). *Educational Research*, Vol. IV, No. 1, pp. 56-61.

examination of a comparatively unexplored area, the relationship of teachers' attitudes towards their pupils' home background and their estimates of pupils' abilities, in order to discover to what extent the difference in reading attainment associated with the socio-economic factor is related to the teachers' attitudes towards the factor itself; (2) an inquiry into marked differences in reading attainment in areas of similar socio-economic status, which takes account not only of differences in method, approach, time of introduction to systematic instruction and sociological conditions affecting material conditions but also the factor of teachers' attitudes and expectations.

It is desired that this research should prove of value to teachers, not only by enabling them to understand more fully the indirect influences affecting their judgments and subsequently their assessments of pupils' readiness and attainment, but also by providing information which will be relevant to them in the day to day effort of tackling the problem of teaching beginners—beginners who need to be viewed, not merely in relation to differences of inherent ability, but also in terms of different backgrounds and varying motivation to learn to read.

Questionnaires

INITIAL QUESTIONNAIRE HEAD TEACHER'S FORM

| Head Teacher

NATIONAL FOUNDATION FOR EDUCATIONAL RESEARCH

Primary School Studies—Teaching Beginners to Read

Name of Head Teacher...

Name of School...Education Division.................

Type of Organization (e.g. Junior Mixed and Infants, Infants only, etc.)

....

Number of infants on roll at end of the Christmas

Term 1958..

Number of reception class teachers...

Address of School..

Telephone No...

Where there is a box answer, would you please tick the appropriate box/boxes.

SECTION A

1. Which of the following reading methods are used in your infant school/department?

alphabetic	phonic	look and say	sentence

Appendix A

2. (a) Does the main approach to the teaching of reading in your infant school/department tend to be

Informal	
Formal	

(b) How would you describe this approach to an interested parent?

3. What would you say are the main considerations which dictate the type of instruction given in your infant school/department?

4. Is the children's interest in reading aroused in any particular way in your infant school/department?

5. In the teaching of reading in your infant school/department does a change of emphasis take place at any stage?

Yes	

No	

Please elaborate your answer

....

6. Would you please indicate the number of teachers in the infant school/department?

(a)

Men	
Women	

Head Teacher

(b)

Under 25 yrs.		25-40 yrs.		40+ yrs.	
married	single	married	single	married	single

(c) Number of teachers who were trained for teaching infants in their college course? ....

(d) Number of teachers who have had more than one year's experience in an infant school/department? ....

SECTION B

1. (a) Is a basic scheme used throughout the infant school/department, e.g. 'Happy Venture', 'Janet and John', 'Beacon', etc.? Please name the scheme or series used.

   (b) Would you please say why this particular scheme or series is used?

   (c) If a basic scheme is used, is it supplemented by readers from other schemes or series? Please name them and say why they are used.

   (d) Would you please estimate the percentage of pupils who, at the end of their infant course, are able to read (as judged by their progress in the basic reading scheme).

Book 4 or beyond	
Books 2 or 3	
Book 1 and below	
	100%

Head Teacher

2. Are children allowed to take their basic readers home?

Yes	
No	

3. (a) Do the teachers in your infant school/ department use reading apparatus?

Yes	
No	

(b) Is this apparatus

published with the readers

made by the teachers?

(c) Is this apparatus used for class purposes: e.g. wall charts, flash cards, etc. for individual purposes, e.g. matching, etc.?

Published apparatus	Teacher made

4. (a) Is there an infant school/department library?

Yes	

No	

Head Teacher

(b) Is there a special room to house it?

Yes [ ]

No [ ]

(c) How is it organized?..

(d) Are children allowed to take library books home?

Yes [ ]

No [ ]

(e) Do

all [ ]

some [ ]

no [ ]

teachers have their own library corners in their class rooms?

(f) What are your sources for obtaining books for either the library or library corners?

5. (a) Are any tests used in your infant school/department? Please name them.

   (b) Would you please say why you use these tests?

6. (a) Do you think the term 'backward' in reading can be applied to children in the infant school?

   (b) What provision, if any, is made for 'backward' readers in your infant school/department?

7. What do you understand by the term 'reading readiness'?

Appendix A

Head Teacher

SECTION C

1. (a) Would you please tick the appropriate space in column A
if your infant school/department has the following:

		A	B
i	A staffroom i		
ii	A hall not used as a canteen or classroom ii		
	A hall used as canteen not class-room		
	A hall not used as canteen but as a classroom		
iii	Large rooms with good windows iii		
iv	Modern chairs and tables in class-rooms iv		
v	Sinks in classrooms v		
vi	Separate stockroom and plenty of cupboards vi		
	No stockroom but cupboards ..		
vii	Electric lighting vii		
viii	Good sanitation and hot water .. viii		
	Good sanitation but no hot water		
	Bad sanitation but hot water ..		
ix	Cloakroom as a special room with pegs and lockers for each child ix		
x	Playground for infants use only .. x		
xi	Good location (e.g. open site, quiet, etc.) xi		
xii	Attractive general appearance .. xii		

(b) Please give the approximate date when the infant school/ department building was erected...

(c) Has this building been enlarged or altered in any way since this date? ....

93

Head Teacher

2. (a) What part do you think a child's home background plays in learning to read? Please elaborate.

3. Would you please indicate by a tick in the appropriate column, in how many of your pupils' families

	Many	Some	Few	Don't know
(a) the mother goes out to work				
(b) the family has its own telephone				
(c) holidays are taken outside the British Isles				
(d) the family has sole use of a garden				

4. *Without questioning the children*, would you please estimate the approximate percentage of your pupils

(a)

who are only children	
who come from a family of 2 children	
,, ,, ,, ,, ,, ,, 3 ,,	
,, ,, ,, ,, ,, ,, 4 ,,	
	100%

94

| Head Teacher |

(b)   whose parents are in the age group

under 25 yrs.	
25-40	
40+	
	100%

5. *Without questioning the children*, would you please indicate the approximate percentage of your present pupils who fall into the following rough classifications of fathers' occupations:

Occupation	%
Professional workers.. ..	
Clerical workers	
Skilled workers	
Semi-skilled workers.. ..	
Unskilled workers	
	100%

6. Have you a parent-teachers' association in the school? If so, would you please describe it briefly.

Yes	

No	

Head Teacher

7. (a) Do you have

a lot of	

some	

not much	

absenteeism?

Would you please give, in order of importance, the types of reasons the children usually have for being absent

....

....

(b) Would you please estimate the approximate percentage of attendance per year?

.... %

(c)

a lot of	

some	

not much	

lateness in the mornings?

Would you please give in order of importance the types of reasons the children usually have for being late............................

....

8. (a) Do you at any time visit the homes of your pupils?   If so, in what circumstances?..

Yes			No	

Head Teacher

(b) Would you please estimate the approximate percentage of parents who come to see you?.. %

Would you please say in what circumstances..

9. (a) Are there any ways in which you are able to judge the level of prosperity of the homes from which your pupils come?

Yes		No	

Please specify..

(b) Do you have any children from 'needy' families, and if so, does the school make any provisions for them?

10. In what ways do parents show their desire for their children to make progress in learning to read?

11. If you have any additional comments, perhaps you would like to add them here..

Would you be willing to co-operate in a further investigation of the problems raised in this questionnaire?

Yes	No

Reading in Infant Classes

INITIAL QUESTIONNAIRE RECEPTION CLASS TEACHER'S FORM

| Reception Class
| Teacher

NATIONAL FOUNDATION FOR EDUCATIONAL RESEARCH

Primary School Studies—Teaching Beginners to Read

Name of Reception Class Teacher...

Name of School..

Size of Class (at the beginning and end of Christmas Term 1958)

....beginning

....end

---

*Where there is a box
answer, would you
please tick the approp-
riate box*

SECTION A

1. (a) Would you please say how many of the children in your
class come from a nursery school/class?

    (b) Have you noticed any differences between these children
and those who have had no nursery experience?

2. Would you please estimate the percentage of your pupils, who
had already begun to read from a book when they first came to
school (i.e. September, 1958)?

    .... %

3. How do you recognize readiness to read in your pupils?

Reception Class
Teacher

4. (a) Which methods do you use in commencing to teach reading?

all	

(b) Is systematic phonic
    instruction given to

some	

pupils?

no	

(c) Please elaborate your answer..

5. Do you use any tests? Please name them.

6. Do you aim at any specific standard before sending your children
   to the next class? (Please specify the standard)

7. (a) Do you systematically follow a published reading scheme/
       series? Please name it.

   (b) If you use a scheme/series, are any children allowed to take
       the basic readers home? (Please give your reasons)

SECTION B

1. Were you trained in infant method in you college course?

....

2. How long have you taught in infant or nursery schools?

....years

3. Have you had any nursery experience? Please give details.

Reception Class Teacher

SECTION C

1. (a) What part do you think a child's home background plays in the initial stages of learning to read? Please elaborate.

   (b) What would you say are the characteristics of a *good* home background?

   (c) What would you say are the characteristics of a *poor* home background?   .

2. Would you please estimate the approximate percentage of children in your class, who usually come to school

with a parent	
with a brother or sister	
with other children	
with a maid or mother's help ..	
with a neighbour or other mother..	
by themselves..	
	100%

3. (a) Do you have

a lot of
some
not much

absenteeism?

   Would you please give in order of importance, the types of reasons the children usually have for being absent.................

Appendix A

> Reception Class
> Teacher

(b) Would you please estimate the approximate percentage of attendance per year?

.... %

a lot of	

(c) Do you have

some	

lateness in the mornings?

not much	

Would you please give in order of importance the types of reasons the children usually have for being late

4. (a) Do you at any time visit the homes of your pupils?

....

In what circumstances?..

(b) Would you please estimate the approximate percentage of parents who come to see you?.. %

In what circumstances? ....

5. Are there any ways in which you are able to judge the level of prosperity of the homes from which your pupils come?

Yes		No	

Please specify..

6. In what ways do the parents of your pupils show their desire for their children to make progress in learning to read?

If you have any additional comments, perhaps you would like to add them here..

1. Statistical Note

By Jill M. Tarryer

General methods of analysis

The main purpose of this report is descriptive and consequently the statistical analysis has been kept as simple as possible. The questionnaire gave rise to data which was largely qualitative, there being only five quantitive variables to consider.

  i   Attainment. Tables VI/2, VII/2.
  ii Age of school building. Table V/1.
 iii Book level at the end of the second year (estimated attainment). Tables VI/3, VII/3.
 iv School material environment. Table V/2.
  v Predicted book level. Table IV/3.

The remaining data were all qualitative and were analysed by extensive use of the χ^2 test.

One way analysis of variance was used to test the differences between school organization and social area means. This method implies the assumption of homogeneity of variance, and for all variables except material environment, the observed data were consistent with this assumption. The standard errors quoted in the text are, therefore, estimates based on either the overall mean square estimate of variance or on the within mean square estimate of variance, dependent on whether or not the means were significantly different.

In the case of material environment, standard errors were computed separately for each mean, and the significance of the observed differences was determined from a joint consideration of the ratios

$$\frac{\overline{X}_1 - \overline{X}_2}{SE_1{}^2 + SE_2{}^2} \qquad \text{and} \qquad \frac{SE_1{}^2}{SE_1{}^2 + SE_2{}^2}$$

where $\overline{X}_1$ and $\overline{X}_2$ are the means of the two groups under consideration, and SE_1 and SE_2 their respective standard errors.

Further details of these methods can be found in the Introduction to *Biometrika Tables for Statisticians*, Volume 1[1].

---

[1] Pearson, E. S. *and* Hartley, H. O., eds. (1958). *Biometrika Tables for Statisticians*, Vol. I. Sections 3·2, 19·1, 9·2, 6·1 and 6·2. Cambridge: Cambridge University Press.

Appendix B

Details of the analysis of head teachers' expectations of book level at the end of the infant course

These statistics were based on Q1. (d) Section B of the Head Teacher's Questionnaire:

> 'Would you please estimate the percentage of pupils who, at the end of their infant course, are able to read (as judged by their progress in the basic reading scheme).'

Book 4 or beyond		(a)
Books 2 & 3		(b)
Book 1 or below		(c)
	100%	

A few of the replies needed slight adjustment on a proportional basis to ensure that the total was 100 per cent. Two ways of analysing the data were employed:

Method 1

The 'estimated mean book level' for each school was derived from the following formula:

Estimated mean book level =

$$\frac{4 \cdot 0 \times a + 2 \cdot 5 \times b + 1 \cdot 0 \times c}{100}$$

where a, b, c were the head teachers' replies as indicated on the right above. These 'Predicted mean book levels' were then treated as school variables, and tests of significance for differences between organizational and social area means were applied as described above.

Method 2

Clearly a more accurate estimate of overall 'mean predicted book level' is obtained if each head teacher's replies are weighted by the number of children in his school. The percentages in Table IV/5 were obtained in this way. The disadvantage of this approach is that tests of significance become rather obscure. However, it can be seen from Table B/1 that in fact the two methods give very similar results and since Method 1 produced nothing significant it is unlikely that Method 2 should do so.

TABLE B/1: *Comparison of Two Estimates of Mean Estimated Book Level. (MEBL)*

	METHOD 1			METHOD 2	
	No. of Schools	MEBL (1)	SE	No. of Children	MEBL (2)
Total	81	3·096	·056	19,622	3·104
Organization					
Infants ..	40	3·195	·079	8,254	3·176
J.M. & I.	41	2·999	·078	11,368	3·051
Social Area					
1 ..	34	3·108	·086	8,637	3·126
2 ..	25	3·103	·100	6,413	3·104
3 ..	22	3·069	·107	4,572	3·062

2. Additional Information and Tables

CHAPTER I

(a) Selection of schools

In 1958 there were 607 primary schools in the London area. It was decided to sample one-in-six of this total population in order to obtain a statistically satisfactory sample of London primary schools. The method used was to first number alphabetically within each type of school organization (infant only and junior mixed and infant) and educational division group of which there were nine, and then using a table of random numbers, the appropriate numbers were randomly chosen from each group; organization and educational division. In this way, the hundred selected schools were chosen so that the numbers of infant only, and junior with infant schools, and also the numbers representing the various divisions of the Authority were directly proportional to the numbers in the Authority as a whole.

A further 20 schools were selected in exactly the same way as the first 100, to have in reserve as a replacement sample, as it was anticipated that some of the selected schools might be unable or unwilling to co-operate. These 20 schools were arranged in a random order with the intention that if replacements were required, they should be taken in that order, rather than automatically replacing the school that had dropped out by another of the same type and from the same district. At the first stage of the investigation, co-operation was sought from the selected 120 schools (original and replacement samples), in completing the initial written questionnaires. Of these schools 71 returned completed questionnaires (59 per cent return). If a school did not answer, a follow-up letter was sent.

It was considered that a larger group than 71 schools was required if the variables, type of school organization and social area were to be controlled. For this reason, it was decided that a further 60 schools should be chosen; but in fact, because of the stratification, it was more convenient to take 61. These were again chosen at random from the whole population with stratification by organization and division. Where a school was selected that was already in one of the two previous samples, another of the same type and division was selected in its place. The final sample of 61 schools was arranged in random order for replacement purposes in the same way as the sample of 20. These further 61 schools were approached and 29 returned completed questionnaires (48 per cent return).

The final group of schools which were used during stage 1 of the research (survey by questionnaire) were as follows:
Original one-in-six sample

of L.C.C. primary schools =	61 co-operated	39 non-responded
1st replacement sample =	10 co-operated	10 non-responded
2nd replacement sample =	29 co-operated	32 non-responded
Total =	100 schools	81 non-responded

Percentage of non-respondents or 'drop-outs' at each stage of the research

Original one-in-six sample = 39 per cent.
1st replacement sample = 50 per cent.
2nd replacement sample = 52 per cent.

Stage I: Survey by questionnaire = 14 per cent.
(schools completing questionnaires, but not continuing with inquiry)

Stage II: Two year inquiry studying 1954 age group children.
Schools who completed first year only = 15 per cent.
Schools who did not complete second year = 12 per cent.

It can be seen from these percentages that the proportion of non-respondents lessened at each stage, and this was related probably to the fact that once personal relationships had been established between the schools and the research team, it was easier to keep in touch with schools and explain the value of their co-operation and individual contribution to the research.

Non-respondents' reasons for not taking part in the research. It was possible to examine the replies of the non-respondents and analyse the reasons they gave for not co-operating. Of the original one-in-six sample, 45 per cent were non-respondents, and 74 per cent of that group gave reasons for their being unable to take part. The most commonly mentioned reasons were:

Shortage of staff or staffing difficulties—(22 per cent of schools).

'Pressure of work'—(18 per cent).

Difficulties particularly in relation to the staffing of the reception class—(18 per cent).

Already taking part in another inquiry—(13 per cent).

The head being newly appointed or about to retire—(13 per cent).

The size of the school—too small or too large—(8 per cent).

Newly opened school—(5 per cent).

Or personal or undisclosed reasons—(13 per cent).

These 60 schools gave 94 reasons for not taking part. There were 21 schools who made no answer to either the original or follow-up letters. Of these 21 schools not replying, eleven were infant only (28 per cent of those schools), and ten junior mixed and infant (24 per cent); eleven were in lower working class areas (35 per cent of those schools), four in working class (18 per cent) and six in middle class areas (21 per cent).

Of the 14 schools completing questionnaires but not continuing with the research, eight gave their reasons for withdrawing which were: two, pressure of work; two, new heads; one, staff difficulties; one, a new school; and two, for other personal reasons.

Of the 25 schools who withdrew during the next two years (stage II), 19 gave reasons which were: one, pressure of work; five, staff difficulties; two, size of school; one, new school; seven, illness or recent appointment of head; three, other reasons.

(b) Comparison of groups of schools at each stage

It was possible to compare the groups of schools co-operating at each stage of the research with one another and with the total group of London schools in relation to the factors of school organization, religious denomination, educational division and social area,

Appendix B

in order to discover how representative the research schools tended to be of London primary schools as a whole. The following comparisons are made between (a) the total London schools, (b) 181 schools originally sampled, (c) 100 schools completing the initial questionnaires, (d) the 86 schools who commenced the two year project, (e) 65 schools completing 2nd year attainment test.

School organization. Table BI/1 shows the distribution of schools by type of organization for the total London schools and each successive stage of the investigation, 1958-1961. Fifteen mixed and infant schools and nine junior girls and infant schools, which were shortly to be reorganized, were omitted from the total group of schools when the one-in-six sample was carried out.

TABLE BI/1: *Type of Organization—Total London Schools and Sample of Schools*

TYPE OF ORGANIZATION	TOTAL LONDON SCHOOLS	181 SAMPLE	100 SCHOOLS	86 SCHOOLS	65 SCHOOLS
Infant only ..	306	93	53	44	31
J.M. & I.	301	88	47	42	34
TOTAL ..	607	181	100	86	65

There was no significant difference between the groups of schools with respect to organization. At each stage, the group of schools selected or co-operating were representative of the total London schools.

Religious denomination. Table BI/2 shows the distributions of schools by religious denomination for the total London schools and the selected and co-operating groups of schools. The schools were classified into three groups: non-denominational, Roman Catholic and Church of England. In the total London schools there were also two Jewish schools, and these were omitted from the London schools before the one-in-six selection of schools took place.

107

TABLE BI/2: *Religious Denomination Total London Schools and Groups of Schools*

RELIGIOUS DENOMINATION	TOTAL LONDON SCHOOLS	181 SAMPLE	100 SCHOOLS	86 SCHOOLS	65 SCHOOLS
Non-Denomination	394	116	71	60	45
Roman Catholic ..	75	22	9	9	6
Church of England	136	43	20	17	14
TOTAL ..	605	181	100	86	65

There was no significant difference between the groups of schools with respect to religious denomination.

Educational division. The London educational service is organized into nine educational divisions for administrative purposes. Table B1/3 shows the distribution of London schools and the groups of schools in relation to this factor. The two Jewish schools were also omitted from the London total schools, as were three schools organized under the county and not in an educational division.

TABLE BI/3: *Educational Division Total London Schools and Groups of Schools*

DIVISION	TOTAL LONDON SCHOOLS	181 SAMPLE	100 SCHOOLS	86 SCHOOLS	65 SCHOOLS
1 ..	68	20	6	5	3
2 ..	69	20	3	2	2
3 ..	57	17	10	8	7
4 ..	43	14	11	10	9
5 ..	59	18	10	9	6
6 ..	65	20	18	15	9
7 ..	78	22	15	14	11
8 ..	80	25	11	9	5
9 ..	83	25	16	14	13
TOTAL ..	602	181	100	86	65

With respect to division, there was no significant difference for the 181 sample, but the 100 sample, the schools completing initial questionnaires, there was a difference significant at 1 per cent.

Divisions 1 and 2 were under-represented, whilst divisions 4 and 6 were over-represented.

Between the 86 schools and the total London schools, the difference was significant at 2 per cent. The difference between the 100 schools completing questionnaires and the 81 non-respondents was significant at 0·1 per cent; the differences between the 86 co-operating schools and the 14 schools who withdrew at the end of stage 1 could not be tested because of small frequencies. Between the 65 schools and the total London schools the trend was less marked. Divisions 1 and 2 remained under-represented but marked over-representation occurred only in division 4 (significance level 5 per cent).

TABLE BI/4: *Observed and Expected Frequencies Based on All London Schools*

EDUCATIONAL DIVISION	100 SCHOOLS		86 SCHOOLS	
	O	E	O	E
1 ..	6	11·3	5	9·7
2 ..	3	11·5	2	9·9
3 ..	10	9·5	8	8·1
4 ..	11	7·1	10	6·1
5 ..	10	9·8	9	8·4
6 ..	18	10·8	15	9·3
7 ..	15	13·0	14	11·2
8 ..	11	13·3	9	11·4
9 ..	16	13·8	14	11·9
TOTAL ..	100	100·1	86	86·0

The highly significant differences between the 100 schools completing questionnaires and the 81 non-respondents can partly be explained by the fact that six schools in division 2 and one school in division 1 were already taking part in a research project being carried out by a higher degree student of the London Institute of Education, but it is not so easy to explain the over-representation of schools from division 6. The highest proportion of respondents was found in this division; only two of the ˳chools who were asked to take part in the research were unable to do so. This division includes a large area south of the river and extends from the lower working class area, through the central working class area, to the outer suburban development.

Social area. Table BI/5 shows the distribution of total London schools and the sample schools according to the three main social areas. The criteria on which this classification was made, the social class distribution within the ward in which the school was situated, were not available for the total London schools. The wards were only obtained for the 181 selected schools.

TABLE BI/5: *Social Area Total London Schools and Sample of Schools*

SOCIAL AREA	TOTAL LONDON SCHOOLS	181 SAMPLE	100 SCHOOLS	86 SCHOOLS	65 SCHOOLS
Lower Working Class	—	69	38	34	24
Working Class ..	—	52	30	24	21
Middle Class ..	—	60	32	28	20
TOTAL ..	—	181	100	86	65

(c) Representativeness of the group of research schools

It can be concluded that the selected schools and the schools at each stage of the research were representative of London primary schools as a whole in relation to type of school organization, religious denomination and social area, but from the time when the co-operating schools completed the questionnaires, the groups of schools were unrepresentative in regard to educational division. This occurred partly because the schools in one particular division were already taking part in another research inquiry, but it is difficult to explain why the schools in one particular division were markedly more enthusiastic and co-operative than those in the other divisions. This division stretched geographically from the inner, older area of development to the outer, most recent suburban areas, but the schools were with one exception classifiable as working and middle class social area schools, so the subject of the research was not of marked appeal to them. However, it may be that because there were fewer lower working class schools, this particular division may have had more stable staffing conditions and, by comparison with other divisions, experienced less of a teacher shortage—the reason most often given for not taking part. Although, when the reasons of the non-respondents were examined by the social area of the school, and the schools who gave no reason were omitted, there appeared to be no significant difference between the schools in the three areas mentioning staffing difficulties or supply teachers as the reason for preferring not to take part.

CHAPTER II

TYPE OF APPROACH

[Head Teacher's Questionnaire—Part A.Q2 (b)]

TABLE BII/1: *Description of Formal/Informal Approach to Teaching Reading—100 Infant Departments/Schools*

TYPE OF APPROACH	DESCRIPTION	TOTAL
Child Centred	Interest is aroused by the teacher using child's *own* interests, experience, and enthusiasm.	30
	No specific method described but stress laid on avoidance of drudgery 'play' learning.	4
	Analytic methods named, no other information.	1
Curriculum Centred	*Teacher* introduces material, mostly through *oral* approach, reading, telling stories.	4
	Teacher introduces material, mostly *visual*, written word, apparatus, skills.	19
	Teacher arouses children's interests using both techniques.	14
	Child's interest aroused by *teacher*, no specific method—'directed' play.	12
	Stress laid on primer from beginning, groups.	5
	Synthetic teaching. Phonic named.	3
Uncodable	No details of approach, e.g. 'I would not explain to a parent'.	7
TOTAL		99
No information		1

TABLE BII/2: *Type of Approach In Child/Curriculum Centred Terms*
100 Infant Departments/Schools

APPROACH	SOCIAL AREA			ORGANIZATION		TOTAL
	1 (N=38)	*2* (N=30)	*3* (N=32)	*Inf.*	*J.M. & I.*	
'Child Centred'	14	11	10	20	13	35
'Curriculum Centred'	21	18	18	30	27	57
No information/ Uncodable	3	1	4	3	5	8
TOTAL	38	30	32	53	47	100

MAIN CONSIDERATIONS
(Head Teacher's Questionnaire—Part A.Q3)

TABLE BII/3: *Distribution of Types of Considerations Named by Heads*
100 Infant Departments/Schools

CONSIDERATION	URBAN						RURAL AND URBAN
	Social Area			Organization		TOTAL LONDON	TOTAL KENT
	1	2	3	Inf.	J.M. & I.		
Needs of individual children	12	9	13	16	18	34	46
Size of class (large), (small)	1	3	4	5	3	8	21
Lack of space	0	1	3	1	3	4	8
Ability of teacher (also interest in method)	7	10	8	15	10	25	5
Other material conditions	0	0	0	0	0	0	0
Maintenance of standards	5	3	4	6	6	12	2
Home background	17	5	6	13	15	28	—
Enjoyment of the use of the skill	3	7	6	11	5	16	—
Children's intelligence	2	1	3	4	2	6	—
Other, e.g. Age-range in reception class	3	3	4	7	3	10	—

Appendix B

Total Number of Items = 143
Mean Number of Items = 1·4
Range of Items   = 1—4

PRINCIPAL METHODS USED TO AROUSE PUPILS'
INTEREST
(Head Teacher's Questionnaire—Part A.Q4)

TABLE BII/4: *Principal Methods Used to Arouse Interest in Learning
to Read*

METHODS	SOCIAL AREA			ORGANIZATION		TOTAL
	1 *(N=36)*	*2* *(N=29)*	*3* *(N=32)*	*Inf.* *(N=52)*	*J.M. & I.* *(N=45)*	*(N=97)*
Labelling	16	14	13	25	18	43
Library facilities ..	10	8	10	20	8	28
Book corners ..	12	12	12	19	17	36
Children's individual interests	12	8	6	14	12	26
News sheets, etc. ..	9	9	4	15	7	22
Projects — teacher organized or topic suggested by teacher	5	4	7	12	4	16
Variety of books ..	13	7	6	11	15	26
Wall stories	7	8	1	11	5	16
Telling, dramatizing stories	9	6	4	9	10	19

Other methods were mentioned by smaller numbers of teachers
but were not included in the above analysis which was confined to
principal methods. These other methods and the number of teachers
mentioning them were as follows:

Talking about pictures in books, children's play, etc., so as to
increase child's vocabulary and hence interest in words (N.12);
use of graded readers or reading cards as records so as to give
children sense of achievement (N.7); teacher's encouragement or
use of incentives, rewards unspecified (N.7); plentiful, useful
apparatus (N.6); home or child made books (N.6); teacher's individual help including hearing children read (N.4); using books as
sources of information, to solve problems, etc., so as to demonstrate
value of acquiring the skill (N.4); recognition of own name or name
cards (N.3); stimulation from older, other children already reading

(N.3); small reward for completion of next book in scheme used as incentive, or reading introductory book to head on completion as reward (N.2); taking book home to read (N.1).

Three heads did not supply this information. Altogether there were 291 methods suggested; mean number 3·0; range 1-8.

CHANGE OF EMPHASIS IN THE TEACHING OF READING
(Head Teacher's Questionnaire—Part A.Q5)

TABLE BII/5: *Comments Made by Heads Who Stated that a Change Did/Did Not Occur—100 Infant Departments/Schools*

Change Did Occur (71 Teachers)

I. *Change occurring in top classes last year higher classes*
    (a) *Phonics* (Formal work)   Totals
        1. Phonics introduced   7
        2. More phonics   8
        3. More formal work along JM & I lines..   2
        4.   ,,   ,,   ,,   at 7 years   2

                                                              19

N.B. Teachers used the terms 'word analysis', 'word building' and 'practice periods' as examples of *formal* work, so these items are included under phonics.

    (b) *Other aspects*
        1. Stress upon progressing through scheme books and additional supplementaries   1
        2. Group work replaced individual work ..   1
        3. Look-and-say used
        4. Comprehension and good expression emphasised   2
        5. More attention paid to the reluctant reader   1
            Change of reading scheme for children making little progress   1
        6. Children tend to make more rapid progress   1

                                                              8   27

II. *Change occurring in the middle of the school half way through
     course*
     (a) *Phonics*   Totals
          1. Phonics introduced 6-6½ years   ..   6
          2. Progress to Look-and-say and Phonics   1
          3. More phonics   4
          4. More formal   2
                                                          ____
                                                           13
                                                          ____
     (b) *Other aspects*
          1. More class reading, intensive   1
          2. Children show an increased desire to
              learn to read   1
          3. Children are encouraged to read for
              information, make use of their skill,
              e.g. reference books/dictionaries   ..   3
          4. Children encouraged to read more
              widely from library books rather than
              primer   2
                                                          ____   ____
                                                           7   20
                                                          ____   ____

III. *Change occurs according to progress of individual
     child*
     (a) *Phonics*
          1. Phonics introduced when child ready,
              changing from Look-and-say to
              Sentence   3
          2. Phonics *introduced* when child reading,
              additional to Look-and-say   5
          3. Phonics *introduced* when child has
              finished Book 2   4
          4. Phonics *introduced* at reading age 6
              years   1
          5. Phonics introduced mental age 7 years   1
          6. More phonics after the introductory
              book   1
          7. More formal work when each child
              reading   2
          8. When child can read attention drawn to
              sounds, use of phonograms and word
              building   4

9. When word building fluent introduced Totals
   to books 1
10. Work becomes more formal/phonics
    (no stage given) 1

———

23

———

(b) *Other aspects*
1. After Phonic and Look-and-say, progress to Sentence 1
2. Individual work in groups when children able to read from a book .. 1
3. Teachers use more than one method,
   emphasise more successful one with
   each child 1
4. Any change depends on individual
   child's progress 1
5. As soon as sounds recognized encouraged to read without sounding letters 1

———   ———

5   28

———   ———

N.B. 71 teachers gave 75 items.

Change Did Not Occur (29 Teachers)
1. Child urged to recognize sounds, letter
   shapes from beginning, visual ap-
   roach 2
2. Child progresses at own pace 5
3. Only for each in regard to first book 2
4. Only that 7-8 year old can say Look-
   and-say words for self 1
5. Interest and effort need to be encouraged all the way 1
6. Only aim is progress to more formal
   work 1
7. Informal throughout whole school .. 1
8. Aim is to have a sustained effort .. 5
9. Only more apparatus used/introduction
   of reader vocabulary 1
10. No answer/teacher new to school .. 11
N.B. The 18 teachers who commented gave 19 items

CHAPTER III

NUMBER OF SCHEMES USED

[Head Teacher's Questionnaire—Part B.Q1 (a)]

TABLE BIII/1: *Number of Schemes Used—100 Infant Departments/ Schools*

SCHEMES	SOCIAL AREA			ORGANIZATION		TOTAL
	1	2	3	Inf.	J.M. & I.	
One scheme only ..	29	23	27	46	33	79
Two schemes ..	7	4	3	4	10	14
Three schemes ..	1	2	0	0	3	3
TOTAL ..	37	29	30	50	46	96
No scheme used ..	1	1	2	3	1	4

TABLE BIII/2: *Heads' Reasons for Choice of Scheme—100 Infant Departments/Schools*

REASONS	TOTAL	RANK ORDER
Scientifically planned, carefully graded vocabulary, progression gradual	50	1
Appeal of pictures, appropriate size of print, format good	46	2
Attractive material, appeals to children's interests, familiar stories, etc.	41	3
Scheme has good supplementary material, apparatus etc.	21	4
Provides practice in familiar words, repetition of vocabulary, etc.	20	5
Popular with staff, choice of teachers	15	6

117

REASONS	TOTAL	RANK ORDER
Books tend to be small in size, not too much repetition	11	7
Supplies phonic material (for Look-and-say approach)	10	8
Need for a change, new scheme	8	
Scheme already in use in school	8	9
Includes both phonic and sentence methods ..	4	11
Means of recording child's progress	3	12
Recommended by Inspector or head teacher, with previous experience of scheme ..	2	13

Total number of items = 239

Mean number of items = 2·4

READING APPARATUS

[Head Teacher's Questionnaire—Part B.Q3 (b), (c)]

TABLE BIII/3: *Type of Reading Apparatus—100 Infant Departments/ Schools*

CATEGORY	SOCIAL AREA			ORGANIZATION		TOTAL
	1	*2*	*3*	*Inf.*	*J.M. & I.*	
Apparatus published with readers ..	0	0	2	1	1	2
Teacher-made apparatus	2	1	5	6	2	8
Both published and teacher-made apparatus	36	29	25	46	44	90
TOTAL ..	38	30	32	53	47	100

TABLE BIII/4: *Purpose(s) for which Apparatus Used—100 Infant Departments/Schools*

PURPOSE	SOCIAL AREA			ORGANIZATION		TOTAL
	1	*2*	*3*	*Inf.*	*J.M. & I.*	
Only for class work	5	6	4	8	7	15
Only with individual children	0	0	1	1	1	2
For both class and individual purposes	33	24	26	43	39	82
TOTAL ..	38	30	31	52	47	99
No information ..	0	0	1	1	0	1

ORGANIZED LIBRARIES

[Head Teacher's Questionnaire—Part B.Q4 (b)]

TABLE BIII/5: *Library Housed in a Separate Room—100 Infant Departments/Schools*

LIBRARY HOUSED IN SEPARATE ROOM	SOCIAL AREA			ORGANIZATION		TOTAL
	1	*2*	*3*	*Inf.*	*J.M. & I.*	
Yes	14	13	11	32	6	38
No	9	10	10	16	13	29
TOTAL ..	23	23	21	48	19	67
No organized library for infants	15	7	11	5	28	33

CHAPTER IV

CHILDREN ABLE TO READ ON ENTRY

(Reception Class Teacher's Questionnaire—Part A.Q2)

TABLE BIV/1: *Estimated Percentage of Pupils Able to Read at Entry—
100 Infant Departments/Schools*

CATEGORY	SOCIAL AREA			ORGANIZATION		TOTAL
	1	*2*	*3*	*Inf.*	*J.M. & I.*	
Few (1–5% able to read)	3	7	4	10	4	14
Some (6–27% able to read)	2	2	0	1	3	4
None (No child able to read from a book on entry)	31	17	26	37	37	74
No information ..	2	4	2	5	3	8

RECEPTION CLASS TEACHERS' STANDARDS

(Reception Class Teacher's Questionnaire—Part A.Q6)

TABLE BIV/2: *Reception Class Teachers Aiming at a Specific Standard
by the End of the Reception Class—100 Infant
Departments/Schools*

CATEGORY	SOCIAL AREAS			ORGANIZATION		TOTAL
	1	*2*	*3*	*Inf.*	*J.M. & I.*	
Teachers with a specific standard ..	12	14	10	14	22	36
No specific standard	26	15	21	38	24	62
No information ..	0	1	1	1	1	2

TABLE BIV/3: *Variety of Standards of Reception Class Teachers (N36)
Setting a Specific Standard—100 Infant
Departments/Schools*

STANDARD DESCRIBED	TOTAL
Introductory book in scheme	8
Introductory book and knowledge of sounds	2
Introductory book, sounds and one supplementary book	2
Introductory book, recognition 40/50 words—basic sight vocabulary	2
Knowledge of basic words in introductory book ..	3
Basic sight vocabulary and two supplementary books ..	1
Introductory book, sounds, recognition 40/50 words ..	1
Introductory and book one	2
Recognize own name, introductory book	2
Good vocabulary/fluency/read well, write etc.	4
Desire to read and some reading routine	1
Part of introductory book, some basic vocabulary ..	1
Book four in scheme	1
Introductory, beginning of book one	1
Knowledge of alphabet, introductory book, book one vocabulary	1
Book one and recognize letters	1
Knowledge of all letter names and sounds	1
Book three in scheme	1
Standard of the lowest group in the class above ..	1
	36

Comments made by 61 teachers answering no specific standard:

Standards dependent on individual child's ability, no class standard set	26
Teacher does not send children to another class, goes up with them	4
Standards not possible as promotion is solely on age and not ability	12
No specific standard expected from infants in their first year, although later a standard may be set ..	3
	55

Six teachers answered that they did not set a standard but did not comment.

TESTS USED IN THE INFANT SCHOOL

[Head Teacher's Questionnaire—Part B.Q5 (a)]

TABLE BIV/4: *Type of Tests Used—43 Infant Departments/Schools*

NAME OF TEST	SOCIAL AREA			ORGANIZATION		TOTAL
	1 (N=17)	*2* (N=16)	*3* (N=10)	*Inf.* (N=20)	*J.M. & I.* (N=23)	
Burt	3	6	2	8	3	11
Schonell	9	8	8	9	16	25
Beacon	1	0	0	1	0	1
Standard Reading Tests	0	1	0	1	0	1
Holborn	4	1	1	2	4	6
Neale Analysis ..	1	0	0	0	1	1
Test, but not named	0	1	0	0	1	1

N.B. 1 Infant and 2 J.M. and I. schools each used two tests.
1 Social Area I, II, III schools each used two tests.

CHAPTER V

MATERIAL ENVIRONMENT

[Head Teacher's Questionnaire—Part C.Q (1)]

Calculation of scores

The schools were assessed on fourteen points and the maximum score was 29.

		Score
1. *Staffroom*		
No		0
Yes		2
2. *Hall*		
No		0
Used both as canteen and classroom		0
Not used as canteen but as classroom		1
Not used as classroom but as canteen		1
Not used as canteen or classroom		2

3. *Classrooms*   *Score*
   No information 0
   Good windows but not large rooms 0
   Some rooms large, all good windows 1
   Large rooms with good windows 2

4. *Equipment*
   No modern chairs and tables 0
   Modern chairs and tables some rooms 1
   Modern chairs and tables 2

5. *Sinks in Classrooms*
   No, or only in one room 0
   Yes, in all or most rooms 2

6. *Stockrooms and Cupboards*
   No separate stockrooms and little cupboard space 0
   No stockroom but cupboards 1
   Separate stockroom and plenty of cupboards . . 2

7. *Electric Lighting*
   No 0
   Yes 2

8. *Sanitation and Hot Water*
   Poor sanitation and no hot water 0
   Bad sanitation but hot water 1
   Satisfactory sanitation but no hot water . . 1
   Satisfactory sanitation and hot water 2

9. *Cloakroom*
   Cloakrooms not adequate 0
   Cloakrooms with pegs only 1
   Pegs and lockers for each child in special room 2

10. *Playgrounds*
    No separate playground 0
    Playground for infants use only 2

11. *Location*

Poor (noisy, etc.) 0
Answer qualified 1
Good (open site, quiet, etc.) 2

12. *Appearance of School*

Unattractive (Gloomy, drab, etc.) 0
Answer qualified (exterior only unattractive) .. 1
Attractive 2

13. *Date of Building*

1840 - 1879 1
1880 - 1919 2
1920 - 1959 3

14. *Alterations*

None or only minor 0
Yes, major 1

TABLE BV/1: *Amenities and Facilities—100 Infant Departments/ Schools*

ITEMS (1–10)	SOCIAL AREA			ORGANIZATION		TOTAL
	1	2	3	Inf.	J.M. & I.	
1. Staffroom						
Yes	37	29	28	51	43	94
No	1	1	4	2	4	6
2. Hall						
Yes	20	10	13	24	19	43
No	2	3	3	3	5	8
As canteen	16	16	16	26	22	48
As classroom	0	1	0	0	1	1
3. Classrooms						
Satisfactory	22	17	20	30	29	59
Some only	3	1	2	5	1	6
Not satisfactory	13	11	10	17	17	34
No Information	0	1	0	1	0	1
4. Equipment						
Modern chairs/tables	33	27	25	43	42	85
Only some rooms	3	1	4	6	2	8
None	2	2	3	4	3	7

TABLE BV/1—*continued*

ITEMS (1–10)	SOCIAL AREA			ORGANIZATION		TOTAL
	1	*2*	*3*	*Inf.*	*J.M. & I.*	
5. *Sinks in Classrooms*						
In most rooms	5	4	8	8	9	17
One or none	33	26	24	45	38	83
6. *Stockrooms and Cupboards*						
Yes	14	18	22	42	22	64
Cupboards only	13	10	10	9	24	33
Unsatisfactory	1	2	0	2	1	3
7. *Electric Lighting*						
Yes	38	30	31	53	46	99
No	0	0	1	0	1	1
8. *Sanitation and Hot Water*						
Satisfactory	26	17	23	33	33	66
Satisfactory sanitation/ no hot water	2	2	3	3	4	7
Poor sanitation/hot water	10	8	3	15	6	21
Unsatisfactory	0	2	3	1	4	5
No information	0	1	0	1	0	1
9. *Cloakrooms*						
Satisfactory	8	7	7	10	12	22
Room with pegs only	18	9	14	28	13	41
Unsatisfactory	12	14	11	15	22	37
10. *Playgrounds*						
Infants use only	17	16	21	36	18	54
No separate playground	21	14	11	17	29	46
11. *Location*						
Good	6	11	17	19	15	34
Qualified	3	2	1	4	2	6
Poor	29	17	14	30	30	60
12. *Appearance*						
Good	9	15	17	22	19	41
Qualified	4	4	3	8	3	11
Poor	25	11	12	23	25	48
13. *Alterations (major)*						
Yes	15	11	11	19	18	37
No	23	19	21	34	29	63

SIZE OF SCHOOL

(Head Teacher's Questionnaire—P.1)

TABLE BV/2: *Size of Infant Department or School—100 Infant Departments/Schools*

CATEGORY			SOCIAL AREA			ORGANIZATION		TOTAL
			1	*2*	*3*	*Inf.*	*J.M. & I.*	
0—49 pupils	..	..	1	1	3	1	4	5
50—99 ,,	..	..	5	7	9	3	18	21
100—149 ,,	..	..	17	7	4	11	17	28
150—199 ,,	..	..	8	6	8	19	3	22
200—249 ,,	..	..	4	4	2	10	0	10
250—299 ,,	..	..	1	5	2	8	0	8
No information	..	..	2	0	4	1	5	6

TEACHER RATIO

[Head Teacher's Questionnaire—P.1 and Part A.Q6 (a)]

TABLE BV/3: *Mean Number of Pupils per Teacher—100 Infant Departments/Schools*

GROUP	MEAN	S.E.
Organization		
Infant only	33·79	9·77
Junior Mixed and Infant	34·48	0·86
Social Area		
Area 1	34·47	0·89
Area 2	35·84	0·98
Area 3	31·74	1·01
TOTAL	34·10	0·57

Appendix B

AGE AND MARITAL STATUS OF STAFF

[Head Teacher's Questionnaire—Part A.Q6 (b)]

TABLE BV/4: *Distribution of Teachers by Age and Marital Status—
100 Infant Departments/Schools*

AGE GROUPS	SOCIAL AREAS			ORGANIZATION		TOTAL
	1	2	3	Inf.	J.M. & I.	
Under 25 years	49	31	33	77	36	113
25—40 years	48	42	39	82	47	129
40+ years	60	62	50	122	50	172

MARITAL STATUS	SOCIAL AREAS			ORGANIZATION		TOTAL
	1	2	3	Inf.	J.M. & I.	
Married	63	65	57	131	54	185
Single	94	70	65	150	79	229

TEACHERS WITH NURSERY EXPERIENCE

(Reception Class Teacher's Questionnaire—Part B.Q.3)

TABLE BV/5: *Reception Class Teachers with Nursery Experience—
100 Infant Departments/Schools*

NURSERY EXPERIENCE	SOCIAL AREA			ORGANIZATION		TOTAL
	1	2	3	Inf.	J.M. & I.	
Yes	10	9	3	10	12	22
No	28	20	28	42	34	76
TOTAL	38	29	31	52	46	98
No information	0	1	1	1	1	2

Reading in Infant Classes

PUPILS WITH NURSERY EXPERIENCE

[Reception Class Teacher's Questionnaire—Part A.Q1 (a), (b)]

TABLE BV/6: *Reception Class Teachers' Observations of Pupils with Nursery Experience—100 Infant Departments/Schools*

Teachers who had noticed no difference	19
Teachers who had noticed differences between nursery and non-nursery children	67
No nursery children/no information ..	12
TOTAL	98
No information	2

Differences Noted Between Nursery and Non-Nursery Pupils—67 Reception Class Teachers

Favourable Differences—(N=48 Mean No. of items 1·6)

Nursery children more sociable, carry out more group play	15
Settle more easily to class work, routine, etc.	15
Show good co-ordination, handle material skillfully.. ..	4
Assume responsibilities readily	5
Show aptitude for reading skills, etc.	5
Are more independent, confident, sensible	30
Are capable of dressing selves	3

Unfavourable differences (N=18 Mean =1·2)

Nursery children are excitable, uninhibited, boisterous, etc.	12
Take longer to settle down, to react to discipline	9

Of the reception class teachers who noted differences between nursery and non-nursery children, 48 described such differences in favourable terms, whilst 18 were unfavourable. One teacher failed to describe the differences observed.

128

Index

130